A Gentle Introduction to (
Programming Fundam

Steven C. Shaffer

About the author

Steven C. Shaffer is a senior lecturer and senior researcher at Penn State University Park, where he has taught software engineering for over a decade. Prior to joining the faculty at Penn State, Dr. Shaffer spent twenty years in industry as a software and quality assurance engineer. He achieved the designations of *Certified Systems Specialist* in 1989 and *Certified Software Quality Engineer* in 1995.

Preface

Programming is fast becoming a basic literacy. Software is pervasive in society and therefore it is needed in virtually every occupation. But for some people, programming feels very unnatural; that's where this book comes in! This book is written in a step-by-step, tutorial style that makes programming available to pretty much anyone who cares to take the time to learn. It's the result of my years of experience and research into teaching introductory programming. In addition, I've used versions of this book in my distance education programming classes for years, which has given me the advantage of optimizing it based on student comments and suggestions.

You can start using this book right away, without buying anything else and without having to install anything on your computer! Within a few days, you will understand the basics of how computer programs work.

C++ is used in this textbook because the syntax is almost exactly the same as C, Java, Javascript, PHP and many other popular programming languages. If you master the concepts in this book, they will transfer to many other languages. In addition, C++ does not require a lot of "scaffolding" to set up. For example, Java requires understanding classes right from the beginning, and PHP requires understanding html. With C++, you start with four standard lines at the top of your program, and you're into the program. Note that I really like Java and PHP, and write in these languages myself quite often; however, for a basic introduction to programming, C++ is the way to go!

When you're finished with this book, the world of programming will be opened up for you; from here, you can go in any direction you wish. Enjoy!

How to use this book

The only way to learn how to program is to *program*! So, the best way to use this book is to sit your Kindle beside you on your desk and type all of the examples and exercises into your compiler and run them. (Details on where to find a compiler are given in chapter 1.)

A note on formatting

Despite my best efforts, some of the program code in the examples wraps around a line in portrait mode (vertical). When this happens, your best approach is to switch to landscape mode (horizontal) on your Kindle; this way, you will be able to see the code lines as they were intended.

Table of contents

-

-

-

-

-

-

-

-

-

-

-

-

•

Chapter 1 — Getting Started

Programming is a way of thinking more than it is a series of facts to learn. Since one of the hardest things to do is to change one's way of thinking, learning to program can be difficult for many students. Some students quickly find it simple and natural, but these are certainly a minority. In order to change your way of thinking and start thinking like a programmer, you will need to practice, practice, practice. This book gives you a way to do that.

Professional software developers often use something called an *Interactive Development Environment* (IDE) when they program; in this book I'm going to suggest that you start out with one of the available on-line code execution web sites. The reason is that sometimes a full IDE can be overwhelming, and you have enough to think about just learning the basics of programming. Additionally, the syntax of the language used in the first 10 chapters of this book can best be described as "C++ light" – as with the professional IDEs, full C++ has thousands of options that the introductory student does not need to worry about. The "C++ light" used here has all of the features of the language that you need to solve interesting small problems; focusing on these aspects of programming allows you to learn the fundamental concepts of programming and avoid being overwhelmed by options. Later in the book, I will give you the step-by-step to learn how to use one of the full scale IDEs that are available for free.

I suggest that the best way proceed is to start up your desktop or laptop computer, set your Kindle down on the desk next to you, and just follow along. There is really no reason to read ahead; programming is about *doing*, not reading.

Your first program

There is a free, web-based code execution program that is very simple to use. There are others as well (do a web search for "online c++ compiler"), but this one is very easy to use while you get started. Alternatively, see for information on downloading and installing a free compiler from Microsoft.

To use the free web-based C++, just follow these steps to get started:

1. Start your web browser.

2. Type `ideone.com` into the address line and press ENTER

3. When the page appears, select the **C++** option on the left (where all the supported programming languages are listed); it should not matter which version number you choose for this introductory book.

4. Type the following program into the text box. I suggest that you type all of the examples in, rather than try to copy/paste them. Doing this will give you a visceral experience of programming and will aid your learning.

```
#include <iostream>
#include <string>
using namespace std;
```

```
int main() {
  cout<<"Hello world!";
  cout<<endl;
  return 0;
}
```

RESULTS
```
Hello world!
```

5. When you've typed all the code, click the SUBMIT button (or, if you're using a different development environment, run the compiler).

6. A new page will be displayed. On this page you will see your code redisplayed, then underneath you will see your output, which is the traditional Hello world! message.

7. If you see an error message in the output box, hit the BACK in your browser and look carefully to make your code *exactly match* the example, including all punctuation and capitalization, etc. More will be said about errors below.

Details are important in programming, so here is a breakdown of the program as shown in the following figure:

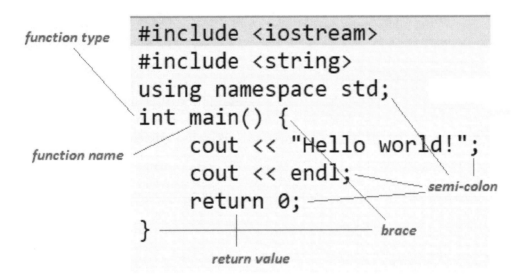

As shown in the diagram, be sure to have the first three lines at the top of every program. These allow you to access the keyboard and the screen, and to use something called *strings* which we will discuss later.

Every program has to have a *function* called main; we will explore functions at great length later in the book, but for now you need to know that a function has a *name* and a *type*. In the example shown, the function name is main, the type is int (short for integer), and the return value is 0 (zero). If you forget to have a main function or accidently misspell the word main, you will see an error such as *undefined reference to 'main'*. Don't worry too much about the details shown here; we will discuss them later in the text; for now, just note that the error says "Your

2

program must contain a main function" and realize that you probably mistyped the name. Fix it and re-run the program.

Most programming lines will end in a *semi-colon*, which usually gives introductory programming students trouble. Formally, every *statement* ends in a semi-colon, but it's hard for new programmers to differentiate what is a statement and what isn't. The best way to learn this is to follow the examples.

Each function begins and ends with a *brace*, which indicates the beginning and end of the function. If you forget a brace at the beginning of the function, you will see an error such as *error: expected initializer before 'cout'*; if you forget a brace at the end of the function, you will see an error such as *expected '}' at end of input*. Note that the first error does not tell you that you are missing a brace; the program does not know what your intentions are, it just knows that something is wrong here. It assumes you wanted to add more program statements, and tells you that it's missing a statement where it expected there to be one. This is very common when programming – only you the programmer know what you intended, the program only knows when something is not right. The "something is not right" here is called a *syntax error*, which means that what you have submitted to C++ is not grammatically correct. It's as though you had said to someone "Whatever else happens, don't forget to" – there needs to be an end to this sentence in order to make sense of it, but no one but you knows what you meant to say!

Every function should end with a `return` statement; however, not every compiler requires it. It's a good idea to get into the habit of including it, though, in case you switch to a compiler that does require it.

Lastly, indentation and other formatting is important in programming, but is usually not enforced by the programming language. The proper way to format a function (and other statements, as we will see later) is to put the opening brace at the end of the first function line (called the function header), then to indent each line inside of the function, until the last line of the function, which contains only the closing brace, lined up underneath the beginning of the function header. Refer back to the code examples above to see the proper alignment. It's important to note that you should indent your program code using the `TAB key`; adding spaces is not sufficient to properly line up your code; it will end up looking different in different editors.

When all goes well and your program works, you will see the output in the "output" box. In this example (refer back to the program), what you have done is to display on the *console output* (`cout`) the specific characters `Hello World!` The term `endl` stands for "end of line" and indicates the end of the output line (more on this later).

Thinking algorithmically

In daily life there is a certain way that people generally think about problems. For example, you might think about how to schedule your day in order to get everything done; this kind of problem is similar to solving a jigsaw puzzle in that you have to balance multiple variables to make them "fit" into a usable form. Although you may have a step-by-step plan of attack, you can not solve the problem entirely sequentially; you have to juggle the pieces to see which ones fit where. For example, a programmed solution to a jigsaw puzzle might look like this:

```
- For each puzzle piece in the bucket, do the following:
-- Pick up every other piece and do the following:
```

3

```
--- For each exposed area of the first puzzle piece, do the following:
---- For each exposed area of the second puzzle piece, do this:
----- If the exposed area of piece #1 fits the exposed area of #2, then:
------- Attach the exposed areas of pieces #1 and #2, and
------- Replace the newly created piece back in the bucket
```

This is called a *brute force algorithm*. An *algorithm* is a step-by-step process which is guaranteed to produce a specific result. Computer programmers use algorithms every day to do their jobs; we will be discussing these at length throughout this book. A brute force algorithm is a process which tries every possible combination to produce a result. Unfortunately, these are rarely an efficient way for a human to solve a problem. For example, if there are 10 puzzle pieces and approximately 4 "exposed areas" (sides) to each piece, then there will be up to 720 combinations to check, just on the first "round" of combining the pieces. Assuming that we have combined the first 10 into chunks of two, leaving 5 pieces for the second "round" of combining, there will be up to another 160 combinations to check. Because we don't know exactly how often we will find two pieces that match, it's difficult to say exactly how many times we will have to compare pieces, but it's easy to see that this is not the way most people would approach solving a 10 piece jigsaw puzzle! However, lacking a more sophisticated algorithm, this is the way a computer would solve the problem; once programmed, a computer could solve even a large version of this problem in a few seconds. But (and here is the kicker), for you to program a computer to do this, you have to learn to think this way.

This is not a test of your intelligence; many very intelligent people are not good programmers; however, since you have undertaken this task (or it has been thrust upon you), you will need to learn how to think this way in order to succeed. To do this, you need to master the following concepts:

- Variables & assignment

- Conditional operation

- Looping

- Functions

- Arrays

In order to "get" programming, you must really, really understand these concepts on a deep level. Luckily, there are only five and, if you spend the time necessary, you will be able to use them to solve a variety of problems.

Problem solving

Programming is inherently a problem solving activity; there are a few simple concepts to learn, but the main task is to figure out how to combine these basic elements to get the answer you are looking for. Programming is a mentally taxing activity, and you will inevitably run into many roadblocks along the way. It is necessary to work through these roadblocks by trying things a different way, and sometimes (aghast!) starting completely over. Do not seek help prematurely; if you do not solve the problem yourself you will not be any closer to being able to solve the next one. And certainly do not copy others' work or seek solutions on the Internet; yes, sometimes you will find them there, but this will not help you. If you wished to learn how to build

4

bookshelves, it would do you no good to go out and buy some; you have to do it yourself to learn it.

Successive refinement

An important aspect of learning to program is to incorporate *successive refinement*, which is done by following these steps:

1. do one small thing that the problem requires;

2. test it;

3. if it does not work, fix it and go back to step 2;

4. if it does work, then go back to step 1.

Continuing to work in this fashion must eventually result in your program being finished. Each time back to step 1 is called an *iteration*, which means one time through a loop. The concept of iteration is central to programming and will be discussed at length later in the text.

The opposite of successive refinement, and a tack that many student erroneously take, is to try to write a program all at once. While this may or may not work for small programs, it will never work for large ones. One can not do everything at once, and yet – despite admonitions to the contrary – students will continue to try this approach. When asked why, some might say that they are in a hurry. Let me be clear: if you are in a hurry (and who isn't?), the best approach to programming is successive refinement. If you wish to spend dozens of unproductive hours programming, then by all means try to write the entire program first and then start testing it.

Overuse of examples

Another mistake students make is to over-use examples. Examples are not magic incantations; they are not meant to solve every programming problem; if such were the case, we would not need programmers anymore! Time and again instructors see "solutions" to problems submitted which are just warmed-over examples from the textbook (or worse, the Internet) which do not solve the given problem at all. The purpose of a programming example is to demonstrate a concept; given a certain goal, here is one way to achieve that goal with a program. Instead of attempting to copy and paste a solution, make sure that you understand the basic structures of programming and then figure out how to use those structures to generate the solution that you are after. Think of a programming language as just that – a language; when you understand the *syntax* (form) and *semantics* (meaning) of the parts of a language, you will be able to create sentences (statements) and paragraphs (programs) which solve the problem at hand.

The context of programming

In the movie *Pirates of Silicon Valley*, the character of Bill Gates says to the inventor of the Altair computer that it is "nothing more than a box with some flashing lights" without (his) software. *Software* is another word for computer program; a *computer program* is a series of commands that a certain computer can understand and interpret. At the lowest level, a computer understands *machine code* – a few basic commands which the computer can execute directly.

Machine code is usually represented in *binary* (base 2) or *hexadecimal* (base 16) and is difficult for humans to interpret and work with. The basic commands that a computer can understand are quite minimal:

- Pull something from memory

- Perform some calculation on something in memory

- Store something in memory

- Go to some place in memory

Although this list is small, everything that is done with computers today, from the simplest toaster to the most complex military application, relies on these basic commands. Of course, when a professional programmer starts to write, for example, a web application, s/he does not start with machine code. Programmers early on decided to write software to help them write software – this led to the construction of assemblers and compilers.

An *assembler* lets the programmer write commands using *mnemonics*: symbols which are easier to read and interpret than machine code (see the figure below). Although these symbols are easier to work with than machine code, they can still more-or-less only execute the basic commands of the computer. So, this made programming easier but not more powerful.

```
        .TITLE   HELLO WORLD
        .MCALL   .TTYOUT,.EXIT
HELLO:: MOV      #MSG,R1 ;STARTING ADDRESS OF STRING
1$:     MOVB     (R1)+,R0 ;FETCH NEXT CHARACTER
        BEQ      DONE    ;IF ZERO, EXIT LOOP
        .TTYOUT          ;OTHERWISE PRINT IT
        BR       1$      ;REPEAT LOOP
DONE:   .EXIT

MSG:    .ASCIZ /Hello, world!/
        .END     HELLO
```

Source: https://en.wikipedia.org/wiki/MACRO-11

Although assembly language is a lot easier to use than machine code, it is still hard to use because the syntax is oriented toward the computer and not toward the programmer. Humans tend to think more abstractly than computers; thus machine code is an example of what is called a *low-level language* because the level of abstraction is low. Sometimes students find this backwards because we tend to think of something that is "low level" as easier than something that is "high level", but in this case the language is difficult to work with because it makes people think like a computer.

Higher-level languages

Realizing the value of assembly language but also its limitations, programmers created higher level languages. One of the earliest high level language was FORTRAN (for Formula Translator). This language allowed programmers to execute statements at a more abstract level. For example, in FORTRAN a programmer can add one to a value as follows:

```
x = x + 1
```

Rather than execute the following series of statements in assembly language:

```
LOAD x INTO R1
ADD 1 TO R1
PUT R1 INTO x
```

Most people agree that the FORTRAN statement is easier to understand. Note, however, that this does not necessarily mean that everyone "gets" it right away. For example, a mathematically sophisticated student might notice right away that no number can equal one more than itself and so, mathematically, the statement $x = x + 1$ is absurd. This highlights the notion that you must understand the *syntax and the semantics* of the programming language you are using.

Syntax and Semantics

The *syntax* of a language is what symbols are allowed, and in what kinds of combinations. For example, the letters `abcdefghijklmnopqrstuvwxyz` are allowed in English, but £ is not. Periods and spaces are needed in certain combinations, whereas the symbol ~ is not. Every language has a syntax, including computer programming languages. Fortunately, the syntax of a program is usually able to be automatically checked by a compiler (discussed below), which incorporates a sort of "spell check" feature. The *semantics* of a language refers to what the symbols mean in certain combinations and contexts. For example, the English word "fire" can mean different things in different contexts. "Ready, aim, fire!" uses a different meaning of fire than "Start a fire" or especially "I'm going to fire you." As mentioned above, the symbol = means something different in different contexts in many programming languages. It's very important to learn the semantics of a programming language, because usually there is no automated way to check the semantics of your program. If your program's syntax is correct but you misunderstand its semantics, you will likely create what's called a *logic error*: this means that your program will run but it will not work as you expected it to. After the first few weeks of programming, most of the troubling errors in your programs will be logic errors.

Compilers

A *compiler* is a piece of software (a program) that converts a program specified in a text file (called the *source code*) into something that can be run on a computer (e.g., machine code). Compilers are specific to particular programming languages (for example, FORTRAN or C++), and are written to run on specific types of computers using particular operating systems. An *operating system* is a piece of software (a program) that takes commands from the user and converts them into actions by the computer. The operating system is what allows images to appear on a computer screen or for a mouse click to open a file. A programmer (a.k.a., you) writes a program (source code) in a text file, then invokes the compiler, which does the following:

- Checks to see if the program is syntactically correct.

- If so, converts it into the detailed code necessary for the program to run on the specific computer and operating system being used.

- (Usually) Allows the user to run the program directly from the compiler's user interface.

The programmer writes the program (source code) in a text file, which is one of the simplest file formats available. A *text file* is a file that is allowed to contain just the basic symbols found on a standard keyboard and a few other "special" characters. On a Microsoft Windows-based machine, you can tell if a file is a text file if it can be opened, read and processed using Notepad (a program that comes free with Microsoft Windows).

Note that a compiler actually creates an *executable file*, which is a file which contains the low-level commands that the computer needs to run the program. If you try to open an executable file using Notepad (for example), you would not be able to recognize anything on the screen. An alternative to a compiler is an interpreter.

Interpreters

An *interpreter* is a program that takes another program (the source code) and performs the actions specified by the source code without creating a low-level executable file first. Note that once a compiler is run on a program, it does not need to be re-run unless the program is changed. This is not the case with an interpreter, which needs to run every time an interpreted program is run. This makes running an interpreted program inherently slower, although with the speed of today's computers the delay is not really noticeable when running most simple applications. The advantage of an interpreter is that certain kinds of run-time checks can be performed. (*Run-time* refers to the time when the program is running.) The kinds of checks that can be performed include making sure the program is not running too long and making sure the program does not try to do anything damaging to the computer. This is especially useful when executing student programs; with a compiled program, a student can sometimes accidentally do damage to the computer s/he is running the program on. This is less likely to be the case with an interpreted program.

Most of the time, C++ is executed using a compiler, such as Microsoft Visual C++ or GCC. As a beginner, it will not matter much to you if you are using a compiler or an interpreter.

The value of practice

Practice is absolutely essential when learning to program. It is not sufficient to simply nod your head at the concepts and believe that you understand them. You must solve problem after problem until the concept becomes second nature to you. In this way, learning to program is like learning any foreign language; you have to use it to become truly fluent in it.

Exercises (solutions are at the end of the book)

Exercise 1.1. Write a program that displays:

```
Hello Universe!
```

Exercise 1.2. Write a program that displays:

```
Hello, there, world!
```

Exercise 1.3. Write a program that displays the following two lines on the screen:

```
Hello there!
How are you?
```

Exercise 1.4. Write a program that displays the following on two lines on the screen:

```
abcdefghijklm
nopqrstuvwxyz
```

Exercise 1.5 Write a program that displays the following on the screen, using two separate cout statements.

```
abcdefghijklmnopqrstuvwxyz
```

Test your understanding

Be sure that you are able to explain the following concepts:

1. Algorithm

2. Brute-force algorithm

3. Successive refinement

4. Iteration

5. Program

6. Machine code

7. Assembly language

8. Low-level language

9. High-level language

10. Syntax

11. Semantics

12. Logic error

13. Compiler

14. Operating system

15. Text file

16. Executable file

17. Interpreter

18. Run-time

Chapter 2 – Variables and assignment

Without variables, a computer is just a calculator. The concept of a variable is at the heart of all computing. A *variable* is a place in computer memory where (potentially changeable) values are stored. This is in contrast to a constant, which never changes value. The number 42, for example, is always equal to 42; it can never have the value 41, 43 or –5463. A variable holds a value, but what that value is can change an unlimited number of times during the execution of a program.

The memory in a computer can be likened to the P.O. boxes at the Post Office. Each box has an address and (potentially) some contents. Let's say you are the postmaster and you have a key for all of the boxes; when you receive a letter for a certain box, you open that box and insert the letter into it, then close it again. Or, if someone asks you for their mail, you can open the proper box and hand them the contents. These are the basic operations of the postmaster (in this scenario):

- Get a piece of mail out of a box.

- Process a piece of mail.

- Put a piece of mail into a box.

The "process" part of the above scenario might involve stamping an envelope, inspecting its contents, etc. (The analogy will inevitably break down at some point.)

A variable has the following attributes:

- A name

- An address

- A value

And you can do the following things with a variable:

- Set (declare) the name

- Get the value

- Change (assign) the value

Using variables in a program

Enter and run the program shown below. This example shows how to declare a variable, assign a value, and display the variable's value on the screen.

```
#include <iostream>
#include <string>
using namespace std;
int main() {
  int x;
```

```
  x = 1;
  cout<<"x is ";
  cout<<x;
  cout<<endl;
  return 0;
}
```

RESULTS
```
x is 1
```

The statement `int x;` tells the program that you want to create a variable called 'x' which has the type 'int' which is short for 'integer'. To return to the post office analogy, this is like someone named "Mr. X" renting a PO box; when a letter comes in for Mr. X, it will go into this box. Within the program, this tells the computer to set aside some memory space for a variable which will be referred to here as `x`.

The statement `x = 1;` tells the program to put the value of `1` into the memory set aside for x. In the post office scenario, this is like delivering a letter to Mr. X. Before you assign a value, the value of the variable is *undefined*, which means that it has no usable value – it is not the same as zero, as students often incorrectly assume. Zero is a valid number; *undefined* is not.

The statement `cout<<x;` tells the program to display the value of `x` on the screen. This is like looking at what Mr. X has in his mail box (remember, you are the postmaster; you have access to everything). When you run this program you will get the result `x is 1`.

Arithmetic statements

Although assigning the value `1` to the variable `x` may have been loads of fun on its own, there is more you can do. C++ allows you to process more complex arithmetic statements so that you can calculate solutions to problems. C++ incorporates addition, subtraction, multiplication and division using the more or- less standard symbols of **+**, **−**, ***** and **/** for addition, subtraction, multiplication and division, respectively. These can be combined using parentheses **( )** to create whatever calculation is needed for the solution. The program below is the same as the one above except that instead of assigning the value of `1` to `x` it instead assigns the value of `1+2`. If you run this program you will get the result `x is 3`. While it's obvious that the programmer could just have put a `3` here, it's for example purposes only.

```
#include <iostream>
#include <string>
using namespace std;
int main() {
  int x;
  x = 1+2;
  cout<<"x is ";
  cout<<x;
  cout<<endl;
  return 0;
}
```

RESULTS
```
x is 3
```

When you program, all arithmetic statements should to be fully parenthesized; doing this makes your intensions explicit. Unfortunately, most compilers don't enforce this, allowing you to accidently calculate the wrong value. The following program shows a more complex calculation in it. Here, the programmer wished to multiply something by 3, although what exactly s/he had in mind is not clear. The reason that the statement is ambiguous is that it is not clear whether the programmer wished the 2 to be multiplied or instead the result of the addition (1 + 2). Should the answer be 7 or 9?

```
#include <iostream>
#include <string>
using namespace std;
int main() {
  int x;
  x = 1+2*3; //<-- AMBIGUOUS
  cout<<"x is ";
  cout<<x;
  cout<<endl;
  return 0;
}
```

The program below shows this problem fixed by using parentheses. Note that this could also have been changed to (1+2)*3, but this would result in a different answer. Remember that when programming, all arithmetic statements should be fully parenthesized to make your intensions clear.

```
#include <iostream>
#include <string>
using namespace std;
int main() {
  int x;
  x = 1+(2*3); //<-- FIXED
  cout<<"x is ";
  cout<<x;
  cout<<endl;
  return 0;
}
```

RESULTS
x is 7

As mentioned earlier, a program that doesn't use variables is little more than a calculator; thus we must be able to use variables in calculations for a programming language to be useful. The following program uses two variables where one is used to calculate the value of the other. Note that the output of this program only shows y is 21 because the only cout statement with a variable in it is cout<<y; however, x still has the value of 10, and if you wanted the value to display you would just need to add a cout<<x; statement to the program.

```
#include <iostream>
#include <string>
using namespace std;
int main() {
  int x;
  int y;
  x = 10;
```

```
    y = 1+(2*x);
    cout<<"y is ";
    cout<<y;
    cout<<endl;
    return 0;
}
```

RESULTS
```
y is 21
```

Assigning variable values based on the variables themselves

Earlier in the text, we discussed that the semantics of programming languages are not the same as standard mathematics (e.g., algebra). The example used at that time was the programming statement `x = x + 1`, which is a common statement in programming. Keep in mind that there is nothing wrong or strange about doing this in programming; it's very common in fact.

Using cin to get values

Computer programs usually need to deal with *input*: data that comes from outside of the program itself. C++ uses the key word `cin` to accomplish this; the following figure shows `cin` in use. When the program reaches the `cin` command, it will wait for a value to be entered. A *prompt* is a request from the program for the user to do something. (When using *ideone.com*, you will need to set this up ahead of time, by typing the data into the "input" textbox.)

```
#include <iostream>
#include <string>
using namespace std;
int main() {
    int x;
    cout<<"Please enter an integer: ";
    cin>>x;
    cout<<"x is ";
    cout<<x;
    cout<<endl;
    return 0;
}
```

For example, if the user enters a `42`, then the result will display as:

```
Please enter an integer:
x is 42
```

The modulus operator (%)

One aspect of programming that students uniformly have trouble with is the modulus operator (`%`). This is a built-in arithmetic operator like `+`, `-`, `*` or `/` and yet it seems to remain a mystery for a lot of students. Use of the modulus operator `%` results in the remainder of an integer division. For example, `9 % 2` is `1` because when you divide nine by two the result is four with a remainder of one. Likewise, `10 % 2` is `0` because when you divide ten by two the result is five with a remainder of zero. Conceptually this is very simple, and yet students consistently have trouble when using this operator. In fact, one of the common questions asked is: why would you ever need such a thing? Consider this: If you take any number and divide it by, for example, `2`, then if the result is zero then the number was evenly divisible by two (a.k.a. and "even" number). If the result of "modding" a number by two is one, then the number is "odd." This kind of processing is useful when writing games and simulations; examples of the use of the modulus operator will be presented later in the text.

Integers versus other data types

The examples in this chapter have used only integers (`int`); in fact, C++ has two other types of data: `float` and `string`. A `float` is a number that can include significant digits to the right of the decimal point. A string is a value that can hold text, such as "Hello World!" or "Abraham Lincoln". Both of these will be explained later in the text. In the following exercises, just use integers.

Exercises (solutions are at the end of the book)

Exercise 2.1. The formula for the volume of a box is `length x width x height`. Write a program that prompts the user for these values and calculates the volume of a box and displays the result. Test with these values: length: 1, width: 2, height: 3, volume (calculated): 6

Exercise 2.2. The formula `C = (F-32) x 5/9` is used for converting Fahrenheit to Celsius. Write a program that prompts for the temperature in Fahrenheit and converts it to Celsius. Note that your solution will be truncated (rounded down) because the variable you will be using is an integer; more will be said about this in a later chapter. Test with these values: fahrenheit: 82, celsius (calculated): 27

Exercise 2.3. Using the information in exercise 2.2, write a program that prompts for the temperature in Celsius and converts it to Fahrenheit. (This will involve stretching your algebra muscles!) Test with these values: celsius: 27, fahrenheit (calculated): 82

Exercise 2.4. The formula for the volume of a sphere is `(4/3) × pi × r^3`. (Note that "r^3" means "r raised to the power of 3". Since you do not know how to raise a number to a power, you can do this by multiplying, i.e., `(r x r x r)`.) Write a program that prompts for the radius and calculates the volume of a sphere and displays the result. Use 3 as the value of PI. Test with these values: radius: 21, volume (calculated): 37044

Test your understanding

Be sure that you are able to explain the following concepts:

1. Variable

2. Constant

3. Undefined

4. Tabs

5. Syntax errors

6. Logic errors

7. Input

8. Prompt

9. Modulus operator

Chapter 3 – More About Variables

In the first chapter you learned how to display text on the screen; however, that is not very useful in that it makes the computer little more than an expensive typewriter. To do anything useful with a computer, you must be able to store and manipulate data. The word data means information for use in calculations, lists, etc. Let's revisit the concept of variables from chapter 2.

The first idea that you will have to understand is why it's called a variable – because its value can vary, as opposed to a constant, where the values stay, well, constant. You are probably familiar with the concept of a variable from algebra; for example, you may have seen an equation like this:

```
12 = 10 + x
```

From this, it is easy to conclude that "x" has the value of 2. Variables in programming languages serve a similar purpose in that they are used as "placeholders" for values. Note, however, that there really is no other possible value for "x" in the equation above – it is pretty much a two and that's all there is to it. However, there is one important difference between variables in programming and variables in algebra: in programming, the values of a variable can change during the execution of the program. The following example shows a variable in a program, similar to what we've seen in chapter 2. This program creates a variable called `age`, sets the value of age to be `21`, then displays it on the screen (after a little introductory text).

```cpp
#include <iostream>
#include <string>
using namespace std;
int main() {
   int age;
   age = 21;
   cout<<"The value of age is ";
   cout<<age;
   cout<<endl;
   return 0;
}
```

RESULTS
```
The value of age is 21
```

Note the following:

1. You have to create a variable before you can give it a value.

2. You have to give the variable a value before you can use that value. (In this example, the only "use" of the value is to display it on the screen. Later on you will be able to use the variables in calculations, etc.)

3. The value 21 in this program is called a *constant* because it never changes.

There are various kinds of variables, called *data types*, each of which is used to store specific kinds of values. The ones that we will be using in this book are as follows:

- Integers: These are whole numbers, typically in the range of –2,147,483,648 to 2,147,483,647. These are declared using the key word **int**.

- Real Numbers: These are numbers with significant digits after the decimal point, usually accurate to about 15 digits. These are declared using the key word **float**.

- Text: This is any sequence of characters that you can find on your keyboard, including such things as "~" and the numerals 0 through 9. These are declared using the key word **string**.

The following example shows a program that uses each of these data types. Note that in order for the compiler to understand where the beginning and ending of your text data is, it needs indicators of some sort. In programming, these are called *delimiters*, and for text data the delimiters are the quotation marks (") on your keyboard. Note that often your computer will generate so-called "smart quotes" as indicated here delimiting the words "smart" and "quotes". If you create a program in a word processor (pretty much a bad idea), make sure that you turn off the smart quotes. Note that you could also prompt the user for the values of these variables; they are hard coded (i.e., the answers are built in) here just to show how the different data types are used.

```cpp
#include <iostream>
#include <string>
using namespace std;
int main() {
  int age = 21;
  float gpa = 3.451;
  string name = "Bob Jones";
  cout<<name;
  cout<<" is ";
  cout<<age;
  cout<<" and has a GPA of ";
  cout<<gpa;
  cout<<endl;
  return 0;
}
```

RESULTS
```
Bob Jones is 21 and has a GPA of 3.451
```

There are other kinds of data types available in most programming languages, but we will not be using those in this introductory book.

Naming your variables

The programming language does not care what you call your variables, but there is good reason to name them properly. Eighty percent of your program's life will be spent in what is called *maintenance*, which means it is being modified. There are few things more annoying than to try to edit a program (either yours or someone else's) and to have all the variables named "j" or something else equally non-descriptive. Get into the habit of naming your variables something descriptive, such as `counter`, `total`, `volume`, etc. Note that since variable names can not contain spaces, you can *not* declare a variable named `interest rate`; instead, a popular option is to call it `interestRate` – using a capital letter in the middle of the name to indicate where a space would be in normal English. Don't start your variable names with a capital letter, and never fully capitalize them.

Forgetting to define or initialize a variable

As mentioned previously, you have to define your variables before assigning a value to them, and you have to assign a value to the variable before you can use it. But what if you forget and don't do this correctly? Then the programming language will give you an error message. For example, what if you forget to define the variable as in the following example? Then you will get an error which says something similar to `error: 'age' was not declared`. Remember that the program only knows what you told it, not what you mean, so sometimes deciphering the error messages can be tricky.

```
#include <iostream>
#include <string>
using namespace std;
int main() {
  cout<<" Age is ";
  cout<<age;
  cout<<endl;
  return 0;
}
```

RESULTS
ERROR!

But what if you instead forgot to give the variable a value before trying to display it? The answer is that it depends on the context and the compiler you are using. For example, the following program tries to display the value of age before it is set (initialized). The compiler might flag this as an error (because you didn't give it an initial value), or it might set it to zero. (Ideone sets it to zero.)

```
#include <iostream>
#include <string>
using namespace std;
int main() {
  int age;
  cout<<" Age is ";
  cout<<age;
  cout<<endl;
  return 0;
}
```

This might seem like the compiler is doing you a favor, but sometimes you can be killed by kindness! Perhaps you meant to set the age, and you don't want the default to be zero. If these lines were buried deep in a program somewhere, you might have a hard time figuring out where the problem was coming from. Thus, it's always a good idea to explicitly initialize your variables when you declare them, as in `int age = 21;`

Run-time errors

If you write a program that is syntactically correct, it may still be wrong. For example, as just discussed, you might forget to give a value to a variable and then try to use it. In this case, if you run the program, your program may crash. A program *crash* means that it stops running. Alternatively, your program could output `The value of pi is 8674645.6393` (or some other invalid number). Other times, your program might just stop running without any indication as to why. All of these are called *run-time errors* because they happen when the program is running (as opposed to when you, say, forget a semicolon or something). A run-time error is always a problem and needs to be fixed. We will discuss other kinds of run-time errors as we progress through the chapters of this book.

Summary

This chapter showed you the basic data types: integer (int), real (float), and text (string). The examples showed you how to make use of them in your programs by declaring and using variables. You also learned about various kinds of programming errors and what causes them.

Exercises

Exercise 3.1. Write a program which asks the user his/her name, stores it in a variable called `name`, and the displays `Hello,` followed by the value of name and an exclamation mark. An example session would look like this:

```
What is your name? Bob
Hello, Bob!
```

Exercise 3.2. Write a program which asks the user his/her last name, stores it in a variable called `lname`, then asks `What is your age?` and stores it in a variable called `age`. After this, the program displays a userid, for example as follows:

```
What is your last name? Jones
What is your age? 20
Your user id is: Jones20
```

Exercise 3.3. Write a program which asks the user his/her major, stores it in a variable called `major`, then asks `What is your GPA?` and stores it in a variable called `gpa`. Next, ask a question based on the answers from the previous two questions. An example session follows; pay attention to how the prompts are spaced.

```
What is your major? Computer Science
What is your GPA? 3.52
Computer Science is very hard;
why do you think you have a GPA of 3.52?
```

Test your understanding

Be sure that you are able to explain the following concepts:

1. Data

2. Variable

3. Constant

4. int

5. float

6. string

7. Delimiter

8. Hard-coding

9. Maintenance

10. Initialized

11. Run-time error

12. Crash

Chapter 4 - Conditional operations

Like people, programs have to be free to make decisions. In addition to variables, the second aspect of all programming languages is the ability to execute decisions based on some condition; these are called conditional operations. A *conditional operation* is a program's ability to follow different paths based on the values of its variables. The most common approach to symbolizing such a decision is the use of an `if` statement; this is written as follows:

```
if (condition) {
   whatever you want to happen
   if the condition is true
}
```

Where `condition` is some comparison, using the comparison operations shown in the figure below. Note especially that "equal to" is symbolized with two equal signs (==) instead of just one; this is to differentiate it from the assignment operator which uses just one equals sign.

>	Greater than
<	Less than
>=	Greater than or equal to
<=	Less than or equal to
!=	Not equal to
==	Equal to
Arithmetic comparison operators	

Note also that a conditional statement uses braces (curly brackets) to group together lines of code, just like you have already been doing within main. A group of program statements joined together by braces is called a *statement block* (meaning a "block" or "clump" of program statements). The following example shows a program using a conditional.

```
#include <iostream>
#include <string>
using namespace std;
int main() {
  int grade;
  cout<<"Enter a grade: ";
  cin>>grade;
  cout<<grade << endl;
  if (grade > 59) {
    cout<<"You passed!";
    cout<<endl;
  }
  return 0;
}
```

RESULTS (run #1)
Enter a grade: 60
You passed!

RESULTS (run #2)
Enter a grade: 58

This program declares a variable called `grade`, gets the value from the user, then tests to see if it is greater than 59; if so, the program displays the message "You passed!". If the grade is *not* greater than 59, then no message is displayed. If you wanted to display the message "You failed!" if the grade was not greater than 59, then your program might look like that shown below. Note that the opposite of >59 is <=59, not just <59; if you were to forget that detail, your program would not work when the user entered 59 (try it!).

```cpp
#include <iostream>
#include <string>
using namespace std;
int main() {
  int grade;
  cout<<"Enter a grade: ";
  cin>>grade;
  cout<<grade << endl;
  if (grade > 59) {
    cout<<"You passed!";
    cout<<endl;
  }
  if (grade <= 59) {
    cout<<"You failed!";
    cout<<endl;
  }
  return 0;
}
```

RESULTS (run #1)
Enter a grade: 60
You passed!

RESULTS (run #2)
Enter a grade: 59
You failed!

More complex examples

Usually a person would not need a computer program to tell if a number was greater than 59, so the example program above is not very interesting. It would be more useful if the program took several grades, calculated the average and then displayed the passed or failed message. The program shown below demonstrates this. In this program, three scores are obtained from the user, and they are added up and divided by three to produce an average.

```cpp
#include <iostream>
#include <string>
using namespace std;
int main() {
  int grade1, grade2, grade3;
  cout<<"Enter the first grade: ";
  cin>>grade1;
  cout<<grade1 << endl;
```

25

```
  cout<<"Enter the second grade: ";
  cin>>grade2;
  cout<<grade2 << endl;
  cout<<"Enter the third grade: ";
  cin>>grade3;
  cout<<grade3 << endl;
  int average =
     (grade1+grade2+grade3)/3;
  if (average > 59) {
    cout<<"You passed!";
    cout<<endl;
  }
  if (average <= 59) {
    cout<<"You failed!";
    cout<<endl;
  }
  return 0;
}
```

RESULTS
```
Enter the first grade: 55
Enter the second grade: 65
Enter the third grade: 75
You passed!
```

Also note, as shown in this example, you can declare more than one variable on a line if you wish; however, all of the variables have to be the same type (in this case, an `int`).

Chaining if statements

In the previous example, there are two `if` statements which happen one after another; this is called a *chain* of `if` statements: where one executes and then the next. In this situation, the results of the first `if` statement do not have a direct effect on the results of the second `if` statement. There can be an indirect effect, however; for example, the following program shows how this can happen.

```
#include <iostream>
#include <string>
using namespace std;
int main() {
  int timeToBoil = -1;
  int temperature;
  cout<<"What is the temperature? ";
  cin>>temperature;
  cout<<temperature << endl;
  if (temperature >= 212) {
    cout<<"How long to boil? ";
    cin>>timeToBoil;
    cout<<timeToBoil << endl;
  }
  if (timeToBoil != -1) {
    cout<<"It will take ";
    cout<<timeToBoil;
    cout<<" minutes to boil.";
  }
```

```
    return 0;
}
```

RESULTS (run #1)
```
What is the temperature? 230
How long to boil? 5
It will take 5 minutes to boil.
```

RESULTS (run #2)
```
What is the temperature? 100
```

Note that in this example, variables are named in upper/lower case combinations such as `timeToBoil`. Since variable names can not contain spaces, programmers use this upper/lower case distinction to mark off word boundaries. This allows you to make your variable names more meaningful.

As programs get more complex you will need to pay closer attention to them in order to understand them. One of the best ways to understand a program is to hand trace it. Hand tracing is the step-by-step execution of a program on paper. The process is difficult to explain in print and is best demonstrated in person or by video; however, we will try here to demonstrate it; get out a piece of paper and follow along step-by-step.

Trace of the "timeToBoil" program:

Place your finger on the first line of the program.
`int main() {`
The program starts executing.
Move your finger to the next line.
`int timeToBoil = -1;`
Space is set aside in memory for an integer called `timeToBoil; the value -1 is stored there.`
Move your finger to the next line.
`int temperature;`
Space is set aside in memory for an integer called `temperature; no initial value is given to this space.`
Move your finger to the next line.
`cout<<"What is the temperature?";`
The prompt is displayed.
Move your finger to the next line.
`cin>>temperature;`
The program gets the value of `temperature from the user (230).`

27

Move your finger to the next line.
`if (temperature >= 212) {`
The program tests to see if the value of `temperature is greater than or equal to 212.`
Since the value of temperature entered is `230, and this is greater than 212, move your finger into the statement block underneath the conditional statement.`
`cout<<"How long to boil?";`
The prompt is displayed.
Move your finger to the next line.
`cin>>timeToBoil;`
The program gets the value of timeToBoil from the user (5).
Move your finger to the next line.
`}`
End of the statement block.
Move your finger to the next line.
`if (timeToBoil != -1) {`
The program tests to see if `timeToBoil is not equal to negative 1.`
Since the value of `timeToBoil entered is 5, and this is not equal to -1, move your finger into the statement block underneath the conditional statement.`
`cout<<"It will take";`
The program displays the words on the screen; note the extra space at the end, so the next thing that is displayed is not smashed up against the word "take".
Move your finger to the next line.
`cout<<timeToBoil;`
Displays the value of `timeToBoil on the screen (5)`
Move your finger to the next line.
`cout<<" minutes to boil.";`
The program displays the words on the screen; note the extra space at the beginning, so the previous thing that is displayed is not smashed up against the word "minutes".
Move your finger to the next line.
`}`
End of the statement block.
Move your finger to the next line.

```
return 0;
```

Ends the program execution.

The output of this program run is: `What is the temperature? How long to boil?`
`It will take 5 minutes to boil.`

Tracing conditions when they do not fire

When a conditional statement is true it is often said to "fire". In the previous example, two conditional statements in the program fired because their conditions were true. The following trace shows an example of the same program executing when both conditions are *not* true and thus do *not* fire. Note the change in the output. This demonstrates how the result of an earlier conditional statement can affect the program flow of later conditional statements; so, even though they are not directly related, they are indirectly related. This can cause some confusion and lead to program errors and/or trouble understanding the results of running a program.

Place your finger on the first line of the program.
`int main() {`
The program starts executing.
Move your finger to the next line.
`int timeToBoil = -1;`
Space is set aside in memory for an integer called `timeToBoil; the value -1 is stored there.`
Move your finger to the next line.
`int temperature;`
Space is set aside in memory for an integer called `temperature; no initial value is given to this space.`
Move your finger to the next line.
`cout<<"What is the temperature?";`
The prompt is displayed.
Move your finger to the next line.
`cin>>temperature;`
The program gets the value of `temperature from the user (100).`
Move your finger to the next line.
`if (temperature >= 212) {`
The program tests to see if the value of `temperature is greater than or equal to 212.`
Since the value of temperature entered is `100,` **and this is less than** `212,` **skip the next statement block and move to the next line after the**

statement block.
`if (timeToBoil != -1) {`
The program tests to see if `timeToBoil is not equal to negative 1.`
Since the value of `timeToBoil` **entered is -1, the condition is not true, so move your finger onto the statement after the conditional statement block.**
`return 0;`
Ends the program execution.

The output of this program run is: `What is the temperature?` **None of the other** `cout` statements are executed, because they exist within a conditional statement block that never executes.

Multi-statement code blocks

As may be obvious from the previous examples, the code blocks that follow a conditional statement can contain multiple lines of code. All of the code between the beginning brace and the ending brace will be executed if the conditional statement is true. But what if the statements inside a code block include more conditional statements? This is the subject of the next section.

Nested code blocks

Code blocks may also be nested. *Nested* means that a code block fully contains one or more other code blocks. Nested code is somewhat like those Russian dolls that fit one inside another. The following example shows a program with nested conditional statements:

```
#include <iostream>
#include <string>
using namespace std;
int main() {
  int x, y;
  cout<<"Enter x: ";
  cin>>x;
  cout<<x << endl;
  cout<<"Enter y: ";
  cin>>y;
  cout<<y << endl;
  if (x > 0) {
    if (y > 0) {
      cout<<"Quadrant I";
    }
    if (y < 0) {
      cout<<"Quadrant IV";
    }
  }
  if (x < 0) {
    if (y > 0) {
      cout<<"Quadrant II";
    }
    if (y < 0) {
      cout<<"Quadrant III";
```

```
      }
    }
  return 0;
}
```

RESULTS (run #1)
```
Enter x: 1
Enter y: 1
Quadrant I
```

RESULTS (run #2)
```
Enter x: -1
Enter y: 1
Quadrant II
```

RESULTS (run #3)
```
Enter x: -1
Enter y: -1
Quadrant III
```

RESULTS (run #4)
```
Enter x: 1
Enter y: -1
Quadrant IV
```

Note the following about the above program:

- For the "Quadrant I" line to execute, *both* of the conditions `x > 0` and `y > 0` have to be true.

- To fully test this program, you have to run it four times (once for each combination of conditions); you should be sure to hand trace this program so that you are certain to understand how it works.

- In this example, I have added lines to display the input back out to the output; this is called *echoing* the input. This is useful if the environment you are using doesn't automatically do this (such as ideone).

- Note also that you can link several `cout` statements together as shown, for example, in the line `cout<<x << endl;` this reduces the number of lines in your program but doesn't effect the readability, as long as you don't run the `cout` statements off of the page!

- If either of the coordinates is zero, then no quadrant is given; this is because the program uses only less than (<) and greater than (>), and never equals-to (==). For practice, type in this program and adjust the program to work with numbers on the axes.

31

Sample problem

Suppose you are given the following problem: You are playing roulette and you always bet the box that indicates "even". Write a program that asks the user for a number. Display "Win!" or "Lose!" based on the results of the roll. Note that a zero (0) loses when you place a bet on either Even or Odd. How would you go about solving this problem? Remember that the best way to write a program is iteratively – that is, do one step, test it, then continue to the next step. Carefully follow the steps shown below, along with an explanation of each step, and build the program step-by-step.

```
#include <iostream>
#include <string>
using namespace std;
int main() {
```

This is how every program starts.

```
int spin;
```

You will need a variable for the result of the spin.

```
cout<<"Enter the spin: "
```

Prompt the user for the value of the spin.

```
cin>>spin;
```

Get the value of the spin from the user.

```
cout<<spin;
```

Display the value of spin on the screen.

```
    return 0;
}
```

Every program ends this way.

Even though the program does not do everything it needs to do, run the program and make sure that this much works. If not, go back and fix it; since the program is relatively short at this point, it should be easy to spot where the program is not working. Once the above code is working, continue adding features to the program as shown below. (New lines are bolded.)

```
#include <iostream>
#include <string>
using namespace std;
int main() {
```

This is how every program starts.

32

```
int spin;
```

You will need a variable for the result of the spin.

```
cout<<"Enter the spin: ";
```

Prompt the user for the value of the spin.

```
cin>>spin;
```

Get the value of the spin from the user.

```
cout<<spin;
```

Display the value of spin on the screen.

```
int mod;
```

Create a place to store the value of the modulus calculation.

```
mod = spin % 2;
```

Calculate spin modulus 2; remember that the modulus operator calculates the remainder of a division; in this case, the remainder of "spin" divided by two.

```
cout<<"Mod is: " << mod;
```

This line displays the value of mod on the screen. Although this line will not be in the final program, it is put there to test that the program is working the way we expect. It's called a trace statement.

```
  return 0;
}
```

Every program ends this way.

Type and run the above changes to your program. When the number 22 (an even number) is entered, the value of mod is 0, when the number 33 (an odd number) is entered, the value of mod is 1. This is as we would expect, since 22 divided by 2 is 11 with a remainder of 0 and 33 divided by 2 is 16 with a remainder of 1. We will use this feature of the modulus operator to tell if we have won or not. (New lines are bolded.)

```
#include <iostream>
#include <string>
using namespace std;
int main() {


```

This is how every program starts.

```
int spin;
```

You will need a variable for the result of the spin.

```
cout<<"Enter the spin: ";
```

Prompt the user for the value of the spin.
`cin>>spin;`
Get the value of the spin from the user.
`cout<<spin;`
Display the value of spin on the screen.
`int mod;`
Create a place to store the value of the modulus calculation.
`mod = spin % 2;`
Calculate spin modulus 2; remember that the modulus operator calculates the remainder of a division; in this case, the remainder of "spin" divided by two.
`cout<<"Mod is: " << mod;`
This line displays the value of mod on the screen. Although this line will not be in the final program, it is put there to test that the program is working the way we expect. It's called a trace statement.

`if (mod == 0) {`
`   cout<<"You win!";`
`}`

If the value of mod is equal to zero, then spin is even and you win.

`if (mod != 0) {`
`   cout<<"You lost!";`
`}`

If the value of mod is not equal to zero, then spin is odd and you lose.
`return 0;` `}`
Every program ends this way.

If you test this programs with the values 22 and 33, you will see that it looks like it's working, more or less. One adjustment we will need to make is to remove the trace statements before finalizing the program. However, there is another, more important issue: what happens in the program when a zero is entered? According to the program specifications above, both even and odd lose if a zero is spun. We need to make accommodations for this, as shown below. Note that this requires that the program use nested conditionals; we only check for even and odd if the spin is not zero. Be sure you understand how the program works by typing it in, running it, and also hand tracing it.

```
#include <iostream>
#include <string>
using namespace std;
int main() {
  int spin;
  cout<<"Enter the spin: ";
  cin>>spin;
  cout<<spin << endl;
  if (spin == 0) {
    cout<<"Zero! Everybody loses!";
  }
  if (spin != 0) {
    int mod;
    mod = spin % 2;
    if (mod == 0) {
      cout<<"You win!";
    }
    if (mod != 0) {
      cout<<"You lost!";
    }
  }
  return 0;
}
```

RESULTS (run #1)
Enter the spin: 21
You lost!

RESULTS (run #2)
Enter the spin: 22
You win!

RESULTS (run #3)
Enter the spin: 0
Zero! Everybody loses!

Another way to do the same thing

The following example shows the same program, except that the second `if` statement has been replaced by the key word `else`. We will discuss the use of `else` in the next chapter.

```
#include <iostream>
#include <string>
using namespace std;
int main() {
  int spin;
  cout<<"Enter the spin: ";
  cin>>spin;
  cout<<spin << endl;
  if (spin == 0) {
    cout<<"Zero! Everybody loses!";
  }
  else {
    int mod;
```

```
    mod = spin % 2;
    if (mod == 0) {
      cout<<"You win!";
    }
    if (mod != 0) {
      cout<<"You lost!";
    }
  }
  return 0;
}
```

RESULTS (run #1)
Enter the spin: 21
You lost!

RESULTS (run #2)
Enter the spin: 22
You win!

RESULTS (run #3)
Enter the spin: 0
Zero! Everybody loses!

Conclusion

Conditional statements are one of the things that differentiate a computer program from a calculator. Making decisions based on the state of the data in your program is a requirement for any but the most trivial of programs. In this chapter you learned how to combine conditional statements in various ways to achieve the desired results.

Exercises

Exercise 4.1. Write a program that asks the user for a test score and determines if it is an "A", "B" etc. based on the following categories:

Range	Result
90 and above	A
80 up to almost 90	B
70 up to almost 80	C
60 up to almost 70	D
anything below 60	F

Exercise 4.2. Write a program that determines a person's health status based on his/her body mass index (BMI). Prompt the user for the BMI and display a message based on the answer as shown in the following chart:

BMI	Result
Less than 18	Underweight
Between 18 and 24	Normal weight
Between 25 and 30	Overweight
31 or greater	Obese

Test your understanding

Be sure that you are able to explain the following concepts:

1. Conditional operation

2. Statement block

3. If statement chain

4. Trace statement

5. Nesting

6. Modulus

7. Iterative development

8. "Firing"

Chapter 5 - More on conditional operations

This chapter introduces some more features of conditional operations, allowing you to develop a bag of tools that you can use to solve more complex programming problems.

Review of relational operators

Recall the list of relational operators from the previous chapter (reproduced below). These are called *relational operators* because they respond to the relationship between what is on the left and what is on the right of the symbol. Note that the symbol for the equals relation (==) is a consistent source of confusion for introductory programming students; it's necessary to use two equal signs because you are *comparing* the values not *assigning* them!

>	Greater than
<	Less than
>=	Greater than or equal to
<=	Less than or equal to
!=	Not equal to
==	Equal to
Relational operators	

Using conditions on strings

An interesting aspect of programming is that you can use relational operators on both numeric and string data. You just have to be sure not to mix up the types. For example, you can test the condition x < y if x and y are both numeric or they are both string, but you can't compare a numeric value to a string value. When comparing string data, your program will do so by comparing the data *lexicographically* – more or less sorted alphabetically, except that all capital letters come before all lower case letters. Thus, BBB comes before bbb and BBB comes before aaa but BBB comes after AAA. In general, if your text is all formatted the same (such as a name starting with a capital letter) then the relational operators will do what you expect with regard to string data. For example, the program shown below shows a rudimentary approach to checking a password. The program has the correct password embedded in it, and it is checked against the value entered by the user. Note also that in this example, the typed password is not displayed on the screen for security purposes.

```
#include <iostream>
#include <string>
using namespace std;
int main() {
  string correctPassword="Charlie378";
  string password;
  cout<<"Please enter your password: ";
  cin>>password;
  if (password == correctPassword) {
    cout<<"Welcome!";
```

```
    }
    if (password != correctPassword) {
      cout<<"Fail!";
    }
    return 0;
}
```

RESULTS (run #1)
Please enter your password: *(correct password entered)*
Welcome!

RESULTS (run #2)
Please enter your password: *(incorrect password entered)*
Fail!

The Else statement

Consider the following program:

```
#include <iostream>
#include <string>
using namespace std;
int main() {
    int age;
    cout<<"How old are you? ";
    cin>>age;
    cout<<age << endl;
    if (age >= 21) {
      cout<<"You are old enough to drink.";
    }
    if (age < 21) {
      cout<<"You are not old enough to drink.";
    }
    return 0;
}
```

RESULTS (run #1)
How old are you? 21
You are old enough to drink.

RESULTS (run #2)
How old are you? 20
You are not old enough to drink.

Even though the program does what it is supposed to do, it is kind of awkward because the test is done twice when really it only needs to be done once. The reason is that if someone is 21 or older (greater than or equal to 21) then s/he can drink, otherwise not. This "otherwise not" is not really captured by the program because we did not utilize an `else` statement, which is adjusted in the following program:

```
#include <iostream>
#include <string>
using namespace std;
```

```
int main() {
  int age;
  cout<<"How old are you? ";
  cin>>age;
  cout<<age << endl;
  if (age >= 21) {
    cout<<"You are old enough to drink.";
  }
  else {
    cout<<"You are not old enough to drink.";
  }
  return 0;
}
```

RESULTS (run #1)
How old are you? 21
You are old enough to drink.

RESULTS (run #2)
How old are you? 20
You are not old enough to drink.

The `else` statement is used to indicate the opposite result of whatever `if` statement it is attached to – note that every `else` statement has to have a corresponding `if` statement, but the reverse is not true. An `if` statement can exist on its own, but an `else` statement cannot. The output for both of these programs is the same because logically these programs are the same; however, as we will see, using the `else` can make programming easier and more error free.

Logical connectives

Sometimes we want to test a condition that depends on more than one variable – for example, we might want to determine if someone is "large" (say, with regard to an airline scat) by determining if they are either tall *or* heavy or perhaps both. Or we might want to buy a house if it has four bedrooms or three bedrooms *and* a den. These kinds of decisions combine variable values based on what are called the *logical connectives* "and" (`&&`) and "or" (`||`). An "and" (`&&`) is true if whatever is to the left is true *and* whatever is to the right is true. An "or" (`||`) is true if whatever is to the left is true *or* whatever to the right is true (*or both*). Note that the `||` is made by holding the shift key and striking the key just below the backspace on most keyboards in the United States.

The following program shows an example of using `||`. The program checks to see if the person is tall (over 75 inches) *or* heavy (over 250 pounds). If a person is 80 inches tall and 200 pounds, the person is tall although not heavy – this makes the test "tall *or* heavy" true because he is at least one of these. Note that this is different than if the program tested for tall *and* heavy (using the `&&` symbol) – in that case, a person who was tall but not heavy would not be offered a larger seat.

```
#include <iostream>
#include <string>
using namespace std;
int main() {
  int height, weight;
```

41

```
cout<<"How tall are you? ";
cin>>height;
cout<<height << endl;
cout<<"How much do you weigh? ";
cin>>weight;
cout<<weight << endl;
if ((height >= 75) || (weight >= 250)) {
  cout<<"You should get a seat with extra room.";
}
else {
  cout<<"You probably don't need extra room.";
}
return 0;
}
```

RESULTS (run #1)
How tall are you? 76
How much do you weigh? 120
You should get a seat with extra room.

RESULTS (run #2)
How tall are you? 80
How much do you weigh? 300
You should get a seat with extra room.

RESULTS (run #3)
How tall are you? 60
How much do you weigh? 250
You should get a seat with extra room.

RESULTS (run #4)
How tall are you? 70
How much do you weigh? 170
You probably don't need extra room.

In order to test this program, there needs to be four runs of the program because there are four possible situations: tall/heavy, tall/not-heavy, not-tall/heavy, and not-tall/not-heavy. The following figure shows all of these possible values and the results of running the program:

Height	Weight	Result
tall	not heavy	extra room
tall	heavy	extra room
not tall	heavy	extra room
not tall	not heavy	**no** extra room
All possible combinations for the program		

You can easily calculate the number of possible significant outcomes by multiplying the number of variables by how many significant values each of them can have; in this case, `weight` can be heavy or not heavy (2 values) and `height` can be tall or not tall (2 values).

42

Thus there are 2×2 or 4 possible significant outcomes. Note that we say *significant* outcomes here because – as far as the program is concerned – there is no significant difference between a height of 74 inches and a height of 1 inch – both place the person in the category of "not tall". Similar logic applies to the categories of tall, heavy, and not heavy. Note that the only way that the statement "tall or heavy" is false is if the person is *neither* tall nor heavy.

If we replace the `||` in the above program with a `&&`, there will be a major change in the results. Using `&&` makes the airline quite miserly with their extra room seats – a non-tall man who weighs 6000 pounds does not even qualify for one! Remember that with an `&&`, *both* the left and the right conditions have to be true for the entire statement to be true.

It's important to note that when you use a logical connective that you need to put parentheses around the conditions on each side of the connective. This makes it clear what things you are trying to connect. For example, this line:

```
if (height >= 75 || weight >= 250)
```

is not as clear as this line:

```
if ((height >= 75) || (weight >= 250))
```

because you could read it as:

```
if (height >= (75 || weight) >= 250)
```

which – surprisingly – is valid in C++ for reasons we can not go into here. Suffice it to say that it is always better to make your meaning perfectly clear by throwing in as many parentheses as necessary to do so.

Truth tables

A *truth table* shows every possible combination of true and false and what the definition of a particular logical symbol is. The truth tables for `&&` and `||` are given below. Read them as follows: the left operand is either true or false; find the two rows that match that value. The right operand is either true or false; find the two rows that match that. Look for the row that matches the left and right truth value, and that row contains the truth value for the whole condition. Thus `X && Y` is true *if and only if* both `X` is true and `Y` is true. Likewise, `X || Y` is false *if and only if* both `X` is false and `Y` is false.

Left side (L)	Right side (R)	L && R
True	True	True
True	False	False
False	True	False
False	False	False
Truth table for `&&` (and)		

Left side (L)	Right side (R)	L || R

True	True	True
True	False	True
False	True	True
False	False	False
Truth table for `||` **(or)**		

More complex logical statements

In real programs, conditional statements can get somewhat complex – not because people like complexity, but because sometimes real life can be complex. Writing software to calculate a car loan, for example, requires dealing with the myriad confusing issues, such as rebates, insurance, etc. So, as you might expect, you can combine complex logical tests into a single if statement. The following program shows an example of this:

```
#include <iostream>
#include <string>
using namespace std;
int main() {
  string company = "Ford";
  if ((company == "GM") || (company == "Ford")
    || (company == "Chrysler")) {
    cout<<"Rebate = $500";
  }
  else {
    cout<<"No rebate";
  }
  return 0;
}
```

RESULTS
```
Rebate = $500
```

Another example of a complex statement is shown below. This program tests to see if a compound is boiling or not, based on three variables: compound, scale, and temp. (Note that water boils a 212 degrees Fahrenheit or at 100 degrees Celsius.) If the scale is Fahrenheit, the temperature has to be at least 212 degrees for the water to boil.

```
#include <iostream>
#include <string>
using namespace std;
int main() {
  string compound = "water";  // Note that these
  string scale = "C";         // values would normally
  int temp = 211;             // be entered by the user
  if ((compound == "water") && (((temp >= 212) && (scale == "F")) || ((temp >= 100)
&& (scale == "C"))))) {
    cout<<"Boiling";
  }
  else {
    cout<<"Not boiling";
```

```
    }
  return 0;
}
```

RESULTS
```
Boiling
```

Note that the text following the `//` symbol is what is called a *comment*; this is a section of text that is meant for humans to read and is ignored by the compiler. In this case, I've added comments so that you realize that these values would normally come from the user; I've set them in the program just to save space and make the examples simpler.

Noting the `if` statement in the program above, getting the details of a complex statement like this is sometimes difficult, so you may want to try using the method shown in the program below.

```cpp
#include <iostream>
#include <string>
using namespace std;
int main() {
  string compound = "water";   // Note that these
  string scale = "C";          // values would normally
  int temp = 211;              // be entered by the user
  if (  (compound == "water") &&
        (  ((temp >= 212) && (scale == "F")) ||
           ((temp >= 100) && (scale == "C"))
        )
     ) {
    cout<<"Boiling";
  }
  else {
    cout<<"Not boiling";
  }
  return 0;
}
```

RESULTS
```
Boiling
```

Here, tabs are used to organize the logical statement into the sub-clauses so you can better see how the clauses are going to combine. In this example, the first clause (compound == "water") is combined with all the other statements with the `&&` connector. The sub-clause that combines the Fahrenheit and Celsius scales is combined with an `||` connector. Inside the sub-sub-clauses, the program checks for the temperature and the scale. When all of this is combined into one `if` statement, the program works properly (try it!).

Summary

In this chapter you learned how to create a program that makes decisions using more complex `if` statements. Although sometimes these decisions are very simple, you can use the logical connectives `&&` and `||` to make complex decisions when necessary. Using `else` allows you to write a program that does one thing in a certain situation, but another if that situation is not the case. Decision making is what differentiates a computer from a simple calculator!

45

Exercises

Exercise 5.1. Re-do exercise 4.1, this time using appropriate logical connectives and else statements to achieve the same results.

Exercise 5.2. Re-do exercise 4.2, this time using appropriate logical connectives and else statements to achieve the same results.

Test your understanding

Be sure that you are able to explain the following concepts:

1. relational operators

2. lexicographically

3. else

4. logical connectives

5. truth table

Chapter 6 - Loops

The main reason why computers have taken over much of modern life is that they are willing to do mundane things over and over again without complaining. The primary way that this happens in a computer program is through the process of *looping*; this chapter introduces you to `while` loops, which work pretty much the same way in most computer languages. A `while` loop executes a block of code over and over while some condition is true. The while loop is written as follows:

```
while (condition) {
  1. Whatever you want to happen while the condition is true
  2. Statement to make sure the loop will terminate
}
```

This looks a lot like an `if` statement, but differs in an important way: the loop body executes forever if the condition remains true. The loop body is the code block under the control of the `while` statement. You have to make sure that there is something in the loop that will eventually make the loop stop running. Here is a simple example:

```
#include <iostream>
#include <string>
using namespace std;
int main() {
  int counter = 1;
  while (counter < 10) {
    cout<<counter << "-";
    counter = counter + 1;
  }
  cout<<endl;
  cout<<"After the loop, counter = ";
  cout<<counter << endl;
  return 0;
}
```

RESULTS
```
1-2-3-4-5-6-7-8-9-
After the loop, counter = 10
```

In this program, a variable named `counter` is initialized to 1, then the `while` statement is encountered. The program asks "Is counter less than 10?" Since it is, the loop body is entered. Inside the loop body, the program displays the value of `counter`, then a dash (-), and **this is important**, *adds 1* to `counter`. The reason that this is important is that it moves the program closer to completion. If, for example, the program instead *subtracted* 1 from `counter`, the program would be moving *further away* from completion. Your loops should always be moving toward completion. The variable `counter` in this example is called the *loop control variable*: the variable whose value controls whether or not the loop body will execute. The output of this program is:

```
1-2-3-4-5-6-7-8-9-
After the loop, counter = 10
```

48

Even this simple program demonstrates some interesting aspects of loops. Note, for example, that the displayed counter never shows 10. This is because the program checks to see if `counter` is *less than* 10 before entering the loop body. When the value of counter is 9, the loop body is entered. The value of counter is displayed, then 1 is added to counter. This makes counter equal to 10, which as we know is not *less than* 10, and thus when the loop re-tests the condition it is not true and the loop body is not executed any more. Note also that `counter` has the value of 10 after the execution of the loop; that is why the program exited the loop.

What would happen if we forgot the second line of the loop body? This is a classic case of an *infinite loop*: a loop whose condition is never false and thus never ends. Be careful! Although Ideone has an execution time max of 5 seconds (which you can boost to 15), in my experience an infinite loop will "hang" the web page. If you are using another environment (such as Visual Studio), you would have to interrupt the process yourself (usually by hitting the control-C combination on your keyboard). If you can see your output, you might be able to tell that the loop control variable was not being changed (or that it was going the wrong way), and thus you could debug your program. To *debug* a program means to remove errors from it. An infinite loop is a common example of a program "bug" which just means an error made by the programmer.

Loops allow you to create much more sophisticated programs; however, in this chapter we will do some basic looping in order to ensure that you have a firm grasp of the concepts before moving to more sophisticated programming in the next chapter. Be sure to work through each of the following examples so that you fully master the basics.

Let's say we want the value of 10 to show up in our loop, based on the program above. One obvious way is change the < into a <= so that the loop will execute one more time than previously:

```
#include <iostream>
#include <string>
using namespace std;
int main() {
  int counter = 1;
  while (counter <= 10) {
    cout<<counter << "-";
    counter = counter + 1;
  }
  cout<<endl;
  cout<<"After the loop, counter = ";
  cout<<counter << endl;
  return 0;
}
```

RESULTS
```
1-2-3-4-5-6-7-8-9-10-
After the loop, counter = 11
```

Note that the number 10 is displayed in the main loop; also note that the value of `counter` after the loop has exited is 11 not 10. What if we did not want counter to be 11 after the loop but instead 10? There could be a good reason for this (as we will see in the next chapter); we might wish to use the value of counter in a calculation following the loop for example. Instead, we could approach this as follows:

```
#include <iostream>
#include <string>
using namespace std;
int main() {
  int counter = 0;
  while (counter < 10) {
    counter = counter + 1;
    cout<<counter << "-";
  }
  cout<<endl;
  cout<<"After the loop, counter = ";
  cout<<counter << endl;
  return 0;
}
```

RESULTS
```
1-2-3-4-5-6-7-8-9-10-
After the loop, counter = 10
```

In this version of the program, we have switched the order of the statements in the loop body; this time `counter` is incremented before the output is written to the screen. The word *incremented* means to have one added to the value of a variable; *decremented* means to have one subtracted from it. This way the `cout` statement shows us the value of `counter` *after* it has already been incremented. Note that this means we have to initialize the value of `counter` to 0 not 1 because otherwise the output would start with `counter is 2` instead of `counter is 1`.

Learning loops with geometric shapes

One way to learn how loops work is to draw simple geometric shapes on the screen. By following along with the following examples you will be able to see how to control what loops do. The following program writes a line of asterisks to the screen in two different ways:

```
#include <iostream>
#include <string>
using namespace std;
int main() {
  cout<<"**********" << endl;
  int counter = 0;
  while (counter < 10) {
    counter = counter + 1;
    cout<<"*";
  }
  cout<<endl;
  return 0;
}
```

RESULTS
```
**********
**********
```

Why we would want to do this will be explained shortly. In the meanwhile, however, be sure to understand how this program works, specifically the loop part. The first `cout` statement just displays ten asterisks on the screen as might be done with a message or any other literal text.

50

The loop instead writes one asterisk ten times; once for each time the loop executes. The following modification shows why this is useful:

```cpp
#include <iostream>
#include <string>
using namespace std;
int main() {
  int width;
  cout<<"Enter the width of the line: ";
  cin>>width;
  cout<<endl;
  int counter = 0;
  while (counter < width) {
    counter = counter + 1;
    cout<<"*";
  }
  cout<<endl;
  return 0;
}
```

RESULTS
```
Enter the width of the line:
******
```

In this example, the user is prompted for the width of the line; s/he could enter 6 (as in the example) or 60 (not shown) and that is how many asterisks would be displayed. You could not do this with a simple cout<<"******"; because you would not know how many asterisks the user would request.

We can now build on this idea to make a square instead of a line. What is a square? It's just an N X N sequence of characters (in this case, asterisks). If we know how to dynamically make a line (as shown above), then all we have to do is to do this same thing N times – well, when you think of doing something N times what do you think of? A loop of course! So, we can nest one loop inside of another as shown below:

```cpp
#include <iostream>
#include <string>
using namespace std;
int main() {
  int rows, cols, size;
  cout<<"Enter size: ";
  cin>>size;
  cout<<endl;
  rows = 0;
  while (rows < size) {
    cols = 0;
    while (cols < size){
      cols = cols + 1;
      cout<<"*";
    }
    cout<<endl;
    rows = rows + 1;
  }
  cout<<endl;
  return 0;
}
```

51

Note that there are two counters – one for the outside loop (the number of rows) and a different one for the inside loop (the number of columns). Also note the strategic placement of the `endl` statement which goes to the next line in the output, which we need in order to get the square to look like a square instead of a line of 36 (6 X 6) asterisks. Also note, though, that because of the vagaries of output displays, a 6-by-6 "square" done in text may not look exactly square on the screen.

It is well worth hand-tracing this program so that you fully understand it; take out a piece of paper and follow along in detail with the program step-by-step, as shown in the previous example.

Sentinel values

The examples up until now have shown loops executing a pre-determined number of times; that is, although based on the user input, by the time the loop starts it is pretty well determined how many times the loop will execute. This is a common, but not the only, use for loops. Sometimes we want to execute a loop until a certain sentinel value is encountered. A *sentinel value* is a special value used to terminate a loop. Often it is a value that is not otherwise valid; for example when dealing with ages the sentinel value might be –1. The program below shows just such a case:

```cpp
#include <iostream>
#include <string>
using namespace std;
int main() {
  int age = 0;
  while (age != -1) {
    cout<<"Enter an age [enter -1 when finished]: ";
    cin>>age;
    cout<<age << endl;
  }
  return 0;
}
```

RESULTS
```
Enter an age [enter -1 when finished]: 1
Enter an age [enter -1 when finished]: 11
Enter an age [enter -1 when finished]: 21
Enter an age [enter -1 when finished]: 31
Enter an age [enter -1 when finished]: 41
Enter an age [enter -1 when finished]: -1
```

Note that this program continues to loop until the user enters a –1 for the age, which then ends the loop. In this case, the –1 is the sentinel value and `age` is the loop control variable. Let's add a feature to this program which counts the number of entries:

```
#include <iostream>
#include <string>
using namespace std;
int main() {
  int age = 0, count = 0;
  while (age != -1) {
    cout<<"Enter an age [enter -1 when finished]: ";
    cin>>age;
    cout<<age << endl;
    count = count + 1;
  }

  cout<<"You entered " << count;
  cout  << " ages." << endl;


  return 0;
}
```

RESULTS
```
Enter an age [enter -1 when finished]: 1
Enter an age [enter -1 when finished]: 11
Enter an age [enter -1 when finished]: 21
Enter an age [enter -1 when finished]: 31
Enter an age [enter -1 when finished]: 41
Enter an age [enter -1 when finished]: -1
You entered 6 ages.
```

Each time through the loop the variable `count` gets incremented. However, there is a problem: if you look at the output, the value of count is six when in fact only five viable ages were entered. That's because the program includes the –1 entry when counting the entries. This is fixed in following program:

```
#include <iostream>
#include <string>
using namespace std;
int main() {
  int age = 0, count = 0;
  while (age != -1) {
    cout<<"Enter an age [enter -1 when finished]: ";
    cin>>age;
    cout<<age << endl;
    if (age != -1) {
      count = count + 1;
    }
  }
  cout<<"You entered " << count;
  cout  << " ages." << endl;
  return 0;
}
```

RESULTS
```
Enter an age [enter -1 when finished]: 1
```

```
Enter an age [enter -1 when finished]: 11
Enter an age [enter -1 when finished]: 21
Enter an age [enter -1 when finished]: 31
Enter an age [enter -1 when finished]: 41
Enter an age [enter -1 when finished]: -1
You entered 5 ages.
```

This program fixes the problem of over-counting the incoming ages by checking to see if `age` is not –1 before counting it. This is a common problem in programming and it is important to remember that it is as simple as surrounding the statement(s) that you don't want to execute with a conditional statement so they will not be executed.

Also note that these programs show a feature of the language wherein you can initialize several variables on the same line as you declare the variables. This is just a convenience feature, but it does shorten your programs and make them somewhat more readable. Just remember that all of the variables declared and initialized this way have to be of the same type.

Enhancing the program further

An additional feature that we can add to the previous program is to report the average age. This is simply a matter of adding up the ages as they come in and – in the end – dividing by the `count`. The following program shows this; be sure to hand-trace the program so you know how it works. Note in particular that the `total = total + age;` line must be within the conditional statement, otherwise the -1 age will be added to total.

```cpp
#include <iostream>
#include <string>
using namespace std;
int main() {
  int age = 0, count = 0, total = 0;
  while (age != -1) {
    cout<<"Enter an age [enter -1 when finished]: ";
    cin>>age;
    cout<<age << endl;
    if (age != -1) {
      count = count + 1;
      total = total + age;
    }
  }
  cout<<"You entered " << count;
  cout  << " ages." << endl;
  int average = total/count;
  cout<<"The average of the ages is ";
  cout  << average << endl;
  return 0;
}
```

RESULTS
```
Enter an age [enter -1 when finished]: 1
Enter an age [enter -1 when finished]: 11
Enter an age [enter -1 when finished]: 21
Enter an age [enter -1 when finished]: 31
Enter an age [enter -1 when finished]: 41
Enter an age [enter -1 when finished]: -1
You entered 5 ages.
```

```
The average of the ages is 21
```

However, this program contains a subtle bug which might not be obvious when you first run it. What if the user enters no valid ages? In other words, what if the first and only age entered is -1? This will make the `count` equal to zero, which is not a valid denominator in a division. In Ideone, you will get the cryptic error message `result: Runtime error time: 0s memory: 2900 kB signal: 8 (SIGFPE)`; in other environments, you will get different errors. To solve the problem, again, all you have to do is write a conditional (if) statement to avoid the problem:

```cpp
#include <iostream>
#include <string>
using namespace std;
int main() {
  int age = 0, count = 0, total = 0;
  while (age != -1) {
    cout<<"Enter an age [enter -1 when finished]: ";
    cin>>age;
    cout<<age << endl;
    if (age != -1) {
      count = count + 1;
      total = total + age;
    }
  }
  cout<<"You entered " << count;
  cout  << " ages." << endl;
  if (count > 0){
    int average = total/count;
    cout<<"The average of the ages is ";
    cout  << average << endl;
  }
  return 0;
}
```

RESULTS
```
Enter an age [enter -1 when finished]: -1
You entered 0 ages.
```

Summary

You may have noticed that the programs are becoming increasingly complex, even for these relatively simple problems. Modern software, even the simple code you're running here, relies on millions of lines of developed code underneath it. There is your program, the compiler, the operating system (e.g., Windows), and the entire Internet structure (if you are using a web-based compiler). All of this code allows you to display some prompts and calculate an average! The point is that it is important to realize that the days of simple software are over; however, the good news is that you can learn to program using a fairly simple interface on top of the work of thousands of programmers working for decades before you.

Loops are the "third leg of the stool" of programming constructs. When you combine variables, conditionals and loops together you can create virtually any program you need. Even though you only know these three basic constructs, they allow enough flexibility to be able to write interesting programs so that you can learn the basic concepts of programming.

Exercises

Exercise 6.1. Write a program that continues to ask the user for a number between one and eleven (inclusive) until the total of the numbers is greater than 21. Be sure to reject any number that is not between 1 and 11 (inclusive). For example:

```
Please pick a number between 1 and 11: 4
Please pick a number between 1 and 11: 12
Out of range; rejected
Please pick a number between 1 and 11: -1
Out of range; rejected
Please pick a number between 1 and 11: 9
Please pick a number between 1 and 11: 8
Please pick a number between 1 and 11: 7
The total is 28
```

Exercise 6.2. Modify the program in the chapter that produces a square to instead produce a triangle of a certain size. The output should look like the example below. This is an example of where you are better off spending more time thinking than typing; you only need to change one or two lines in the program to get the desired effect:

```
Enter size: 5
*
**
***
****
*****
```

Test your understanding

Be sure that you are able to explain the following concepts:

1. loop body

2. loop control variable

3. infinite loop

4. debug

5. increment

6. decrement

7. nest

8. sentinel

Chapter 7 – More complex problems

Students sometimes complain that they understand the pieces of programming, but that they "can't" turn those pieces into completed programs. *Nonsense!* No one is born knowing how to program; it is an acquired skill just like any other skill. The best (and perhaps only) way to learn how to program is to practice, practice, practice!

This chapter is a hodgepodge of various practice problems, along with solutions to those problems. You should try each problem before looking at the solution – looking at a solution and nodding does not involve your mind actively enough; you need to work the problems yourself!

Combining tests, testing string conditions, and using trace statements

The following example shows a program that asks the user a question and continues to ask it until a valid answer is given:

```
#include <iostream>
#include <string>
using namespace std;
int main() {
  string answer = "no answer";
  while ((answer != "yes") && (answer != "no")) {
    cout<<"Please answer 'yes' or 'no': ";
    cin>>answer;
    cout<<"TRACE: [" << answer << "]" << endl;
  }
  cout<<"You answered: " << answer << endl;
  return 0;
}
```

RESULTS
```
Please answer 'yes' or 'no': TRACE: [okay]
Please answer 'yes' or 'no': TRACE: [this]
Please answer 'yes' or 'no': TRACE: [is]
Please answer 'yes' or 'no': TRACE: [my]
Please answer 'yes' or 'no': TRACE: [answer]
Please answer 'yes' or 'no': TRACE: [ yes ]
Please answer 'yes' or 'no': TRACE: [yes]
You answered: yes
```

Note the following:

- You can create more complex conditions for a `while` loop just as you can an `if` statement.

- You can compare strings lexicographically in `while` loops just as you can in `if` statements.

- When creating trace statements, it is often convenient to display text data between two delimiters, such as the square brackets shown. This allows you to see if your data may contain extra spaces, as shown in one of the answers to the prompt in the example.

Note that whereas `while` loops and `if` statements look very similar, you must be careful not to mix them up! A loop is used when the process should execute zero, one or more times (based on the data); a conditional (`if`) statement only executes zero or one time. If you don't want the code block to ever execute more than once, you need to use an `if` statement, not a `while` loop.

Repeated calculations

Loops can be used for many things other than asking a question over and over. For example, a common use of a loop might be to display the steps in a loan pay-off as with a car loan or a mortgage, as shown here:

```
#include <iostream>
#include <string>
using namespace std;
int main() {
  float loanAmount, monthlyPayment;
  int numMonths;
  cout<<"Enter the loan amount: ";
  cin>>loanAmount;
  cout<<loanAmount << endl;
  cout<<"Enter the months to pay off: ";
  cin>>numMonths;
  cout<<numMonths << endl;
  monthlyPayment = loanAmount / numMonths;
  while (loanAmount >= monthlyPayment) {
    cout<<"Payment: $" << monthlyPayment << endl;
    loanAmount = loanAmount - monthlyPayment;
  }
  cout<<"Final payment: $" << loanAmount << endl;
  return 0;
}
```

RESULTS
```
Enter the loan amount: 9999
Enter the months to pay off: 12
Payment: $833.25
Payment: $833.25
Payment: $833.25
Payment: $833.25
Payment: $833.25
Payment: $833.25
Payment: $833.25
Payment: $833.25
Payment: $833.25
Payment: $833.25
Payment: $833.25
Payment: $833.25
Final payment: $0
```

Note the following things about this program:

- The user is prompted for the loan amount and the number of months on the loan. The monthly payment is calculated by dividing the loan amount by the number of months.

In the example above, the amounts work out evenly, but that might not be the case (see below).

- The `loanAmount` is the loop control variable (LCV) in this example because `loanAmount` is lowered each time through the loop by subtracting the monthly payment from it. Thus, each time the loop is executed the LCV will come closer to being true; if not, then the loop would be headed the "wrong way" and never stop.

- Note that, whereas `loanAmount` and `monthlyPayment` are stored as `float`, `numMonths` is stored as an `int`, because there is no fractional part of a number of months (at least in this application).

- The dollar sign ($) is included in the output simply by putting it to the screen in front of `monthlyPayment` — there is no special "currency" type.

Spiral development

Once a program becomes too complex to simply write the first time through, the appropriate method is to use a *spiral development* approach — write something, test it, fix it (if necessary), test it again and, if it works appropriately, go on to add more features. This is the best way to make forward progress on your programs; you should always be able to add "one more thing." The unfortunate alternative is what is called *analysis paralysis*, which is the condition of not being able to start the program because you are overwhelmed with the size or complexity of the task. Always start with something that you know you can do — perhaps just displaying the prompts — and then add from there. Be sure to test each iteration through your development cycle, because you don't want too get far into your development and find out that there is an error in something that you did at the beginning. In the rest of this chapter we will be enhancing the above program and learning new things as we go.

The first thing that we might notice is that our program does not work very well if the numbers don't work out "evenly":

```
#include <iostream>
#include <string>
using namespace std;
int main() {
  float loanAmount, monthlyPayment;
  int numMonths;
  cout<<"Enter the loan amount: ";
  cin>>loanAmount;
  cout<<loanAmount << endl;
  cout<<"Enter the months to pay off: ";
  cin>>numMonths;
  cout<<numMonths << endl;
  monthlyPayment = loanAmount / numMonths;
  while (loanAmount >= monthlyPayment) {
    cout<<"Payment: $" << monthlyPayment << endl;
    loanAmount = loanAmount - monthlyPayment;
  }
  cout<<"Final payment: $" << loanAmount << endl;
  return 0;
}
```

RESULTS
```
Enter the loan amount: 999.97
Enter the months to pay off: 12
```
```
Payment: $83.3308
Payment: $83.3308
Payment: $83.3308
Payment: $83.3308
Payment: $83.3308
Payment: $83.3308
Payment: $83.3308
Payment: $83.3308
Payment: $83.3308
Payment: $83.3308
Payment: $83.3308
Payment: $83.3308
Final payment: $4.57764e-05
```

There are two problems here: (1) The payment has too many decimal places, and (2) the final payment is displaying in scientific notation. In order to fix both of these problems, you need to do two things:

1. Add a line near the top to include the "iomanip" library, which contains a bunch of tools to manipulate I/O (input/output).

2. Insert the line `cout<<std::fixed << std::setprecision(2);` anywhere near the top of the program.

Here are the changes, in bold:

```
#include <iostream>

#include <iomanip>
#include <string>
using namespace std;
int main() {

  cout<<std::fixed << std::setprecision(2);
  float loanAmount, monthlyPayment;
  int numMonths;
  cout<<"Enter the loan amount: ";
  cin>>loanAmount;
  cout<<loanAmount << endl;
  cout<<"Enter the months to pay off: ";
  cin>>numMonths;
  cout<<numMonths << endl;
  monthlyPayment = loanAmount / numMonths;
  while (loanAmount >= monthlyPayment) {
    cout<<"Payment: $" << monthlyPayment << endl;
    loanAmount = loanAmount - monthlyPayment;
  }
  cout<<"Final payment: $" << loanAmount << endl;
  return 0;
}
```

RESULTS
```
Enter the loan amount: 999.97
Enter the months to pay off: 12
```

```
Payment: $83.33
Payment: $83.33
Payment: $83.33
Payment: $83.33
Payment: $83.33
Payment: $83.33
Payment: $83.33
Payment: $83.33
Payment: $83.33
Payment: $83.33
Payment: $83.33
Final payment: $0.00
```

This looks better, but, if you do the math, you will find that there is a penny missing. This is because the program is rounding all floating point outputs to the nearest hundredths place. While this is convenient for the display, it means that errors can result. In order to understand where the missing penny went you have to first understand the difference between integers (int) and real numbers (float). In a computer, integers can be stored precisely because they are *discrete* values – that is, they do not have fractional parts. Real numbers, stored as `float`, on the other hand, are stored approximately. In most situations the answers are "close enough" and do not cause any trouble; however, with some numbers you can introduce rounding errors into a program if you are not careful. In the movie Office Space, for example, the employees of a company contrive to steal all the rounding errors from company transactions. Whereas it's certainly possible to fix the program to avoid the rounding errors, it would add a needless distraction here, and so we shall move on, noting that this can be a problem in a production system.

Still more to fix

The astute programmer will know to try various, unusual, combinations of data when testing a program. In an earlier program we saw the results of a divide-by-zero error. (Recall that dividing by zero leads to an undefined, or infinite, result in mathematics.) The following program adds a trace statement which identifies a strange behavior of the program:

```cpp
#include <iostream>
#include <iomanip>
#include <string>
using namespace std;
int main() {
  cout<<std::fixed << std::setprecision(2);
  float loanAmount, monthlyPayment;
  int numMonths;
  cout<<"Enter the loan amount: ";
  cin>>loanAmount;
  cout<<loanAmount << endl;
  cout<<"Enter the months to pay off: ";
  cin>>numMonths;
  cout<<numMonths << endl;
  monthlyPayment = loanAmount / numMonths;
  cout<<"monthlyPayment = " << monthlyPayment << endl;
  while (loanAmount >= monthlyPayment) {
    cout<<"Payment: $" << monthlyPayment << endl;
    loanAmount = loanAmount - monthlyPayment;
  }
```

```
    cout<<"Final payment: $" << loanAmount << endl;
    return 0;
}
```

```
Enter the loan amount: 999.97
Enter the months to pay off: 0
monthlyPayment = inf
Final payment: $999.97
```

It might surprise you that this program seems to work properly, since if there are zero months to pay off the loan, the final payment (that is, right now), will be the full amount of the loan. In this case, the value of `monthlyPayment` shows as `inf`, which is short for "infinity". Looking at the `while` statement, we see that it will execute while the loan amount is greater than or equal to the monthly payment. Well, since the monthly payment is infinite, the loan amount will never be greater than (or equal to) it. So, the `while` loop never fires, and the final payment is the same as the original loan amount.

Although we "lucked out" in this situation, it's important to remember that different programming environments will act differently to certain errors. Thus, it's important to identify the possible problems and fix them explicitly, rather than waiting to see if it passes testing. In this case, a better version of this program is:

```
#include <iostream>
#include <iomanip>
#include <string>
using namespace std;
int main() {
    cout<<std::fixed << std::setprecision(2);
    float loanAmount, monthlyPayment;
    int numMonths;
    cout<<"Enter the loan amount: ";
    cin>>loanAmount;
    cout<<loanAmount << endl;
    cout<<"Enter the months to pay off: ";
    cin>>numMonths;
    cout<<numMonths << endl;
    if (numMonths > 0) {
        monthlyPayment = loanAmount / numMonths;
        while (loanAmount >= monthlyPayment) {
            cout<<"Payment: $" << monthlyPayment << endl;
            loanAmount = loanAmount - monthlyPayment;
        }
    }
    cout<<"Final payment: $" << loanAmount << endl;
    return 0;
}
```

```
Enter the loan amount: 999.97
Enter the months to pay off: 0
Final payment: $999.97
```

A note about code segments

As the programs we are writing become increasingly complex, it is expedient sometimes to just show the few lines that we are discussing rather than to reproduce the entire program. As you gain knowledge of programming you will be able to see where these items refer and how they should be fit into your program. As you are reading the subsequent chapters, be sure to type these programs into whatever compiler you're using, run them, and test the results – this is the only way that you will be sure you understand the material.

Exercises

Exercise 7.1. Write a program that asks the user for integers; stop when the user enters a zero (0). For each nonzero number, count how many even, odd, positive and negative values are entered. Display the results as shown below:

```
Enter a number: -1
Enter a number: 1
Enter a number: -2
Enter a number: 2
Enter a number: -3
Enter a number: 3
Enter a number: 0
You entered:
2 even numbers
4 odd numbers
3 positive numbers
3 negative numbers
```

Exercise 7.2. Write a program that asks the user for points on a graph. Determine what quadrant the points are in and display an appropriate message. Ask if the user wants to continue, and if the answer is "Yes" then continue; otherwise do not. Count how many points were in each quadrant and display the count at the end. If the point is on either axis, display a message and do not count it. A sample run is shown below.

```
Enter x: 1
Enter y: 1
Quadrant I
Continue ('Yes' or 'No')? Yes
Enter x: -1
Enter y: 1
Quadrant II
Continue ('Yes' or 'No')? Yes
Enter x: -1
Enter y: -1
Quadrant III
Continue ('Yes' or 'No')? Yes
Enter x: 1
Enter y: -1
Quadrant IV
Continue ('Yes' or 'No')? Yes
Enter x: 0
Enter y: 100
Axis points are skipped
Continue ('Yes' or 'No')? No
Quadrant I had 1 point(s)
Quadrant II had 1 point(s)
Quadrant III had 1 point(s)
Quadrant IV had 1 point(s)
```

Test your understanding

Be sure that you are able to explain the following concepts:

1. Practice

2. Lexicographically

3. Trace statement delimiters

4. LCV

5. Spiral development

6. Analysis paralysis

7. Discrete values

8. Divide by zero error

Chapter 8 – Functions

After the brief time you've been studying programming, it has probably become apparent that even a relatively simple program can require many lines of code. You can imagine what it's like for professional software developers who must manage millions of lines of code. Without some way to organize the code, very quickly the programs become too complex to maintain, and errors begin to be inserted into the program. One of the basic ways to organize your code is the use of a *function*, which is a relatively small piece of code which does one particular thing of moderate complexity.

If you take even a relatively simple program such as those shown in previous chapters, you can see that they're getting somewhat unwieldy. There is too much going on in main for one to follow the entire process; this leads to errors when modifying the program and even unforeseen errors in the first version of the program. A good strategy for beginning programmers is to *modularize* your programs as you develop them, which means that you will take sections of code from `main` and move them into their own functions as each section is written and tested. A *function* is a segment of code that you can use from multiple places in your program. Before you can do that, though, you need to learn the mechanics of writing a function. You need to know the following to write a function:

- The name of the function.

- What the parameters are.

- What the function does.

- What the return type is.

Here is a small program which incorporates a simple function:

```cpp
#include <iostream>
#include <iomanip>
#include <string>
using namespace std;

float calcTax(float price) {
  float tax;
  tax = price * 0.06;
  return tax;
}

int main() {
  float price, salesTax, total;
  cout<<std::fixed << std::setprecision(2);
  cout<<"Enter price: ";
  cin>>price;
  cout<<price << endl;
  salesTax = calcTax(price);
  total = price + salesTax;
  cout<<"The total is $ ";
  cout<<total << endl;
  return 0;
}
```

```
Enter price: 9.98
The total is $ 10.58
```

Note the following about this program:

- There is a function named `calcTax`.

- The function has one parameter, a `float` named `price`.

- The function calculates `tax` based on 6% of `price`.

- The function returns the `tax` amount to the part of the program that *calls* it (in `main`).

- In this example, the returned value is "caught" by the variable `salestax` in `main`, where it is used to calculate the `total` amount.

The best way to understand how functions works is by hand-tracing an example:

Hand trace of the program

Place your finger on the first line of the program.
`int main() {`
The program starts executing.
Move your finger to the next line of the program.
`float price, salesTax, total;`
Space is set aside in memory for floats called `price, salesTax and total.` `On your paper, write the words` **price, salesTax,** `and` **total** `and write the word undefined underneath each.`
Move your finger to the next line of the program.
`cout<<std::fixed << std::setprecision(2);`
Sets the display precision to 2.
Move your finger to the next line of the program.
`cout<<"Enter price: ";`
The program prompts the user for the price.
Move your finger to the next line of the program.
`cin>>price;`
The program obtains the value of `price from the user.` `On your paper, cross out the word undefined underneath price and replace it with 9.98.`
Move your finger to the next line of the program.
`cout<<price << endl;`

The value of `price is displayed on the screen.`

Move your finger to the next line of the program.

```
salesTax = calcTax(price);
```

The program will call the function `calcTax by "jumping" to the function in the code.`

Move your finger to the first line of `calcTax`.

```
float calcTax(float price) {
```

This line states that the function `calcTax receives a float called price and will return (send back) a float.`

Move your finger to the next line of the program.

```
float tax;
```

Space is set aside in memory for a `float called tax. On your paper, write` *the word* **tax** *and write the word* `undefined` *underneath it.*

Move your finger to the next line of the program.

```
tax = price * 0.06;
```

The program will multiply `price times 0.06 and place the value into the` *variable space for tax. On your paper, cross out undefined underneath tax and write* **0.5988**.

Move your finger to the next line of the program.

```
return tax;
```

The program will now jump back to where it was called from (main), sending the value of tax back with it.

Move your finger to where `calcTax was called from`.

```
salesTax = calcTax(price);
```

The program will now take the thrown back value (0.5988) and put it into the variable space for `salesTax. On your paper, cross out undefined underneath` `salesTax and write` **0.5988**.

Move your finger to the next line of the program.

```
total = price + salesTax;
```

The program adds the value of `salesTax to price and puts the result in` `total. On you paper, cross out the word undefined underneath total` *and write in* **10.5788** *instead.*

Move your finger to the next line of the program.

```
cout<<"The total is $ ";
```

The program displays the words `The total is $ on the screen.`

Move your finger to the next line of the program.

> *The program displays the value of* `total` *(rounded to 2 decimal places) on the screen.*

Move your finger to the next line of the program.

```
return 0;
```

> *We can now understand this line (see below)! The program terminates.*

Why there is a return statement at the end of the program

Since the beginning of the book you have been including a `return` statement at the end of each program without any real explanation. The reason was that you did not know anything about functions at the time. The explanation is now clear: if you look at how `main` is defined, you will see that it is obviously a function; it has no parameters and it returns an `int`. Thus `return 0;` is a way of completing the requirement that a function has to return a value of the appropriate type. In professional programming environments, your `main` function might send a status value (an `int`) back to the operating system when the program terminates, to let the other processes know if it exited okay, contained an error, etc. The line `return 0;` is standard practice when you are not concerned with sending a message back to the operating system.

Back to the example

In the example, one can make the argument that there is no need for the function, since the calculation is so simple. (Remember though that it is primarily there to show the mechanics of writing a function.) However, what if the function was modified to also calculate the tax for states other than Pennsylvania? An extended version is shown below, where New Jersey and Delaware are included, making the function more complicated and thus more "worthy" of being in it's own function.

```cpp
#include <iostream>
#include <iomanip>
#include <string>
using namespace std;

float calcTax(float price, string state) {
  float tax;
  if (state == "PA") {
    tax = price * 0.06;
  }
  if (state == "NJ") {
    tax = price * 0.07;
  }
  if (state == "DE") {
    tax = price * 0.06;
  }
  return tax;
}

int main() {
  float price, salesTax, total;
```

```
  string state;
  cout<<std::fixed << std::setprecision(2);
  cout<<"Enter price: ";
  cin>>price;
  cout<<price << endl;
  cout<<"Enter state: ";
  cin>>state;
  cout<<state << endl;
  salesTax = calcTax(price, state);
  total = price + salesTax;
  cout<<"The total is $ ";
  cout<<total << endl;
  return 0;
}
```

RESULTS
```
Enter price: 9.98
Enter state: NJ
The total is $ 10.68
```

In real applications, calculating sales tax is quite complex due to the varying laws of different states (and possibly different countries). Imagine just what would be required here for the 50 United States; although not "complex: (it's just a bunch of `if` statements), it is long and unwieldy and thus is a good candidate for making into a separate function. Also, it's quite likely that this tax calculation would be needed somewhere else in the program and there is no need to write and maintain it in more than one place.

Note that if there is more than one parameter, you must separate them with commas.

One thing to keep in mind when running the program: if the value of `state` is not one of the choices tested for, the program will either throw a run-time error or default the sales tax to zero. This is because tax is never assigned a value unless the state is either PA, NJ or DE. For example, if the user types `Pa` instead of `PA`, then the sales tax might show as zero, which would cause a lot of problems when the state comes to collect its share! Note also that run-time errors a program shows are not always easy to interpret; it takes patience and experience to be able to understand all of the errors a programming language can display.

The best approach is to make sure that the program catches the error, as shown below:

```
#include <iostream>
#include <iomanip>
#include <string>
using namespace std;

float calcTax(float price, string state) {
  float tax = -99999;
  if (state == "PA") {
    tax = price * 0.06;
  }
  if (state == "NJ") {
    tax = price * 0.07;
  }
  if (state == "DE") {
    tax = price * 0.06;
  }
```

```
  if (tax == -99999) {
    cout<<"ERROR! State [";
    cout<<state << "] not found!";
    cout<<endl;
  }
  return tax;
}

int main() {
  float price, tax, total;
  string state;
  cout<<std::fixed << std::setprecision(2);
  cout<<"Enter price: ";
  cin>>price;
  cout<<price << endl;
  cout<<"Enter state: ";
  cin>>state;
  cout<<state << endl;
  tax = calcTax(price, state);
  total = price + tax;
  cout<<"The total is $ ";
  cout<<total << endl;
  return 0;
}
```

RESULTS
```
Enter price: 9.98
Enter state: Pa
ERROR! State [Pa] not found!
The total is $ -99989.02
```

There are more subtle ways to handle this, but this quick fix gets the job done! Whoever is running the cash register will immediately figure out that something is wrong.

Scope of variables

Notice another change in the above program; the variable salesTax in main has been renamed to just tax. Note also that in the calcTax function there is also a variable named tax. It's **very important to understand that these are different variables**, even though they have the same name. This is an example of what is called variable scope in programming. The *scope* of a variable is the length of time or place that a variable lives, usually restricted to when a function is executing.

When calcTax is called, the variable tax is created; this is called a *local* variable. When the function returns, that variable ceases to exist. The variables in main exist throughout the execution of the program because main continues to execute until the program is finished running.

Note though that you can not access variables in main from within other functions, unless they are explicitly passed to the function. For example, the following program will *not* compile:

```
#include <iostream>
#include <string>
using namespace std;
```

```cpp
float tryMe(int x, int y) {
  cout<<x << endl;
  cout<<y << endl;
  cout<<oops << endl;
  return (x+y);
}

int main() {
  int x = 1, y = 2;
  float answer, oops = 3.1415;
  answer = tryMe(x, y);
  cout<<answer << endl;
  return 0;
}
```

RESULTS
```
prog.cpp: In function 'float tryMe(int, int)':
prog.cpp:9:10: error: 'oops' was not declared in this scope
```

Pass by value

The following example shows a nonsense program that demonstrates an important point: when you pass a parameter into a function, changes to that parameter will *not* be reflected when the function goes back where it came from. In the example, the variable x is initially set to 11, then passed to the function `tryMe`. Once in `tryMe`, the program displays the value (still 11) then adds one to x. The value (now 12) is displayed on the screen, and the function returns to `main`. In `main`, the value of x is once again displayed, but it has its original value (11).

```cpp
#include <iostream>
#include <string>
using namespace std;

int tryMe(int x) {
  cout<<"In tryMe, x is " << x << endl;
  x = x + 1;
  cout<<"Now in tryMe, x is " << x << endl;
  return x;
}

int main() {
  int x = 11;
  cout<<"In main, x is " << x << endl;
  int answer = tryMe(x);
  cout<<"Now in main, x is " << x << endl;
  return 0;
}
```

RESULTS
```
In main, x is 11
In tryMe, x is 11
Now in tryMe, x is 12
Now in main, x is 11
```

73

Sometimes this is surprising to newcomers to programming, but consider the alternative. The following shows the same program, but the literal number 11 is passed to tryMe. If the program allowed the parameter to be changed, this would mean that the literal number 11 would now have the value of 12! Clearly, this does not make any sense, and so it is not allowed.

```
#include <iostream>
#include <string>
using namespace std;

int tryMe(int x) {
   cout<<"In tryMe, x is " << x << endl;
   x = x + 1;
   cout<<"Now in tryMe, x is " << x << endl;
   return x;
}

int main() {
   int x = 11;
   cout<<"Now in main, x is " << x << endl;
   int answer = tryMe(11);
   cout<<"Now in main, x is " << x << endl;
   return 0;
}
```

RESULTS
```
Now in main, x is 11
In tryMe, x is 11
Now in tryMe, x is 12
Now in main, x is 11
```

This aspect of programming is called *pass by value*: it means that the *values* of the variables are passed to the function, not the actual variables. (Remember that a variable is shorthand for a space in memory.) The space set aside for x in main is not affected by the changes to the space set aside for the x in tryMe. In fact, internally they do not even have the same name; instead of both being x they are called main_x and tryMe_x respectively.

Return values

To further complicate the matter, notice that in the above program, the result of the return value from tryMe is placed into a variable called answer, and then ignored. In the example below, a small change makes a *big difference* with regard to the output of the program. In this program, x "catches" the return value of tryMe and in this way the value of x is changed. Note that this does not violate the rules laid out above; the change actually happens in main (not tryMe) because the x is on the left side of an assignment operator in main. This is the way that the result of a function call can be used in the calling function (in this case main). This is necessary of course because it would be pointless to call a function if you could not make use of the result.

```
#include <iostream>
#include <string>
using namespace std;

int tryMe(int x) {
```

```cpp
  cout<<"In tryMe, x is " << x << endl;
  x = x + 1;
  cout<<"Now in tryMe, x is " << x << endl;
  return x;
}

int main() {
  int x = 11;
  cout<<"Now in main, x is " << x << endl;
  x = tryMe(11);
  cout<<"Now in main, x is " << x << endl;
  return 0;
}
```

RESULTS
```
Now in main, x is 11
In tryMe, x is 11
Now in tryMe, x is 12
Now in main, x is 12
```

A common misconception

The above examples show the parameters having the same name as the variables that are being passed, and this is a common device when introducing parameters. However, this leads to a common misconception with beginning programmers: that the parameters of a function must have the same names as the variables that you are passing in. *Nothing could be further from the truth.* For example, what if you needed to calculate the following formula:

$$\frac{x^2 + y^2}{2.0}$$

The following program solves this. (Note that you could adjust the program to prompt for x and y, but this method is shorter and simpler for purposes of demonstration).

```cpp
#include <iostream>
#include <string>
using namespace std;

float square(float value) {
  float answer = value * value;
  return answer;
}

int main() {
  float x = 11.1, y = 12.2;
  float xSquared, ySquared, answer;
  xSquared = square(x);
  ySquared = square(y);
  answer = (xSquared+ySquared)/2.0;
  cout<<answer << endl;
  return 0;
```

75

```
}
```

Clearly, if you are going to have a function called `square`, you can not name the parameter the same as the variable that will be passed (say `x`), otherwise you would only be able to use it on that one variable! So, if you want to be able to create generally useful functions, you should name the parameters something descriptive but generic.

Removing intermediate variables

As useful as the above program is, it is also somewhat clumsy. Having intermediate variables in your program can sometimes make your program easier to read, but sometimes they can just clutter it up. The following program does the same thing as the one above, except that the extra variables `xsquared` and `ysquared` have been eliminated. This is possible due to the fact that you can embed function calls right into a calculation, as shown. This program is somewhat easier to read because it is a more "natural" expression of the original formula.

```cpp
#include <iostream>
#include <string>
using namespace std;

float square(float value) {
  float answer = value * value;
  return answer;
}

int main() {
  float x = 11.1, y = 12.2, answer;
  answer = (square(x)+square(y))/2.0;
  cout<<answer << endl;
  return 0;
}
```

RESULTS
136.025

Building on other functions

Let's say we have the function `square` from above available, and we need a function called `fourth` which raises a variable to the fourth power. Of course, we could build a new function entirely from "scratch"; however, modern software is built by judiciously utilizing functions that have already been written. Thus, the following example shows a new function called `fourth` which itself calls the already-written function `square`.

```cpp
#include <iostream>
#include <string>
using namespace std;

float square(float value) {
  float answer = value * value;
```

```
  return answer;
}

float fourth(float value) {
  float answer = square(value) * square(value);
  return answer;
}

int main() {
  float x = 2.2, answer;
  answer = fourth(x);
  cout<<answer << endl;
  return 0;
}
```

RESULTS
```
23.4256
```

Although this is a simple example, it demonstrates that you can create a structure or stack of functions which can be called to solve more-and-more complex problems. We will see more examples of this in the next chapter.

Order matters

The following shows a program with an error. This program is the same as that shown above, except that the function `fourth` appears *above* the function `square`. Note that the program that processes your program (called a parser) reads your program from the top down. When processing (parsing) the function `fourth`, it encounters a reference to `square` which it does not recognize. This highlights the fact that you have to *define* a function before you can *call* it. This is similar to a variable, which you have to declare before you can reference it.

```
#include <iostream>
#include <string>
using namespace std;


float fourth(float value) {
  float answer = square(value) * square(value);
  return answer;
}

float square(float value) {
  float answer = value * value;
  return answer;
}

int main() {
  float x = 2.2, answer;
  answer = fourth(x);
  cout<<answer << endl;
  return 0;
}
```

RESULTS
```
prog.cpp: In function 'float fourth(float)':
```

```
prog.cpp:7:32: error: 'square' was not declared in this scope
```

Summary

In this chapter you learned how to write functions, which is important to understand since it is the building up of a "toolkit" of functions that really gives modern software it's power.

Exercises

Exercise 8.1. Functions can return a `string`, not just an `int` or a `float`. Write a function called `evenOrOdd` which takes an integer parameter and returns either "Even" or "Odd" based on the value passed. In `main`, prompt the user for a number, called `num`, then pass `num` to `evenOrOdd` and display the returned value on the screen. Keep doing this until the user enters a zero. Use the following run as an example:

```
Enter a number: 11
Odd
Enter a number: 12
Even
Enter a number: 13
Odd
Enter a number: 0
```

Exercise 8.2. Create a function called `sumTo` which takes an integer parameter and returns the total of all of the numbers from 1 to that number. For example, if the user entered a 5, the function would calculate 1 + 2 + 3 + 4 + 5 = 15. Keep prompting the user for a number until a zero (0) is entered. Use the following run as an example:

```
Enter a number: 5
15
Enter a number: 25
325
Enter a number: 100
5050
Enter a number: 0
```

Test your understanding

Be sure that you are able to explain the following concepts:

1. function

2. modularize

3. return value

4. parameter

5. scope

6. pass by value

7. parser

Chapter 9 – An extended example

The following extended example is designed to help you in two ways: (1) to better your understanding of the use of functions and (2) to better your understanding of how to develop more complex programs in general. Toward this second purpose, this extended example shows a series of steps, each getting us closer to the goal of the completed program. This approach, called *spiral development*, is used whenever a program is too complex to write "off the cuff" – which is most programs once you have passed the simplest examples. *To get the most out of this example, you must follow along, typing in the code as you go!*

First, let us begin with the problem definition: Write a program that utilizes the distance formula to calculate the distance between two points on a plane. Prompt the user for the x and y co-ordinates of the points. The distance formula is given as follows:

$$d = \sqrt{(x_2 - x_1)^2 + (y_2 - y_1)^2}$$

The sample output is as follows:

```
Enter the x coordinate for point 1: 5
Enter the y coordinate for point 1: 5
Enter the x coordinate for point 2: -5
Enter the y coordinate for point 2: -5
The distance is 14.14
```

The first response for some students when faced with this problem is to panic. But, as is often the case, panic is not helpful here. Instead the student should focus on what s/he does know how to do, and start with that. The following example shows the beginnings of a program to do something like what is required, although only the prompts are working.

```cpp
#include <iostream>
#include <iomanip>
#include <string>
using namespace std;

int main() {
  cout<<"Enter the x coordinate for point 1: ";
  cout<<"Enter the y coordinate for point 1: ";
  cout<<"Enter the x coordinate for point 2: ";
  cout<<"Enter the y coordinate for point 2: ";
  return 0;
}
```

```
RESULTS (all running together)
Enter the x coordinate for point 1:
Enter the y coordinate for point 1:
Enter the x coordinate for point 2:
Enter the y coordinate for point 2:
```

Next we need to get the values from the user. In the example in the problem description the points are integers, so we know what type we need to make the variables. The following shows the next iteration of the program:

```
#include <iostream>
#include <iomanip>
#include <string>
using namespace std;

int main() {
   int x1, y1, x2, y2;
   cout<<"Enter the x coordinate for point 1: ";
   cin>>x1;
   cout<<x1 << endl;
   cout<<"Enter the y coordinate for point 1: ";
   cin>>y1;
   cout<<y1 << endl;
   cout<<"Enter the x coordinate for point 2: ";
   cin>>x2;
   cout<<x2 << endl;
   cout<<"Enter the y coordinate for point 2: ";
   cin>>y2;
   cout<<y2 << endl;
   return 0;
}
```

RESULTS
```
Enter the x coordinate for point 1: 5
Enter the y coordinate for point 1: 5
Enter the x coordinate for point 2: -5
Enter the y coordinate for point 2: -5
```

Since the program is already starting to take up a lot of real estate in `main`, let's create a function called `distance` which will accept the four coordinates and return the distance:

```
#include <iostream>
#include <iomanip>
#include <string>
using namespace std;


float distance(int x1, int y1, int x2, int y2) {
   return 12.34;
}

int main() {
   int x1, y1, x2, y2;
   cout<<"Enter the x coordinate for point 1: ";
   cin>>x1;
   cout<<x1 << endl;
   cout<<"Enter the y coordinate for point 1: ";
   cin>>y1;
   cout<<y1 << endl;
   cout<<"Enter the x coordinate for point 2: ";
   cin>>x2;
   cout<<x2 << endl;
   cout<<"Enter the y coordinate for point 2: ";
   cin>>y2;
```

```
  cout<<y2 << endl;
  float dist = distance(x1, y1, x2, y2);
  cout<<"The distance is ";
  cout<<dist << endl;
  return 0;
}
```

RESULTS
```
Enter the x coordinate for point 1: 5
Enter the y coordinate for point 1: 5
Enter the x coordinate for point 2: -5
Enter the y coordinate for point 2: -5
The distance is 12.34
```

Note that we know that the coordinates (the parameters to the function) are integers and we can pretty much surmise that the return value for the function (the distance) will be a float. So, we "dummy up" the answer and get just part of the program working; of course, it is unlikely that every pair of coordinates we enter will have the distance of 12.34, but we just use this as a stepping stone toward the final result.

What is needed now is to calculate the distance between the points. If you are not very familiar with either programming or math, this might seem daunting – thus you should do what we have done so far, which is to do *something* that you know how to do; in this case, addition and subtraction. Note that the "inner most" part of the distance formula shows the subtraction of $x1$ from $x2$ and $y1$ from $y2$, so we do that next. Since we don't really know what these intermediate values represent, we just call them diffx and diffy. Since $x1$, $y1$, $x2$, and $y2$ are all integers, diffx and diffy can both be integers without the fear of the loss of precision. In order to check what is happening, we include some trace statements; in the end we will delete these.

```
#include <iostream>
#include <iomanip>
#include <string>
using namespace std;

float distance(int x1, int y1, int x2, int y2) {
  int diffx, diffy;
  diffx = x2-x1;
  diffy = y2-y1;
  cout<<diffx << " vs ";
  cout<<diffy << endl;
  return 12.34;
}

int main() {
  int x1, y1, x2, y2;
  cout<<"Enter the x coordinate for point 1: ";
  cin>>x1;
  cout<<x1 << endl;
  cout<<"Enter the y coordinate for point 1: ";
  cin>>y1;
  cout<<y1 << endl;
  cout<<"Enter the x coordinate for point 2: ";
  cin>>x2;
  cout<<x2 << endl;
  cout<<"Enter the y coordinate for point 2: ";
```

83

```
  cin>>y2;
  cout<<y2 << endl;
  float dist = distance(x1, y1, x2, y2);
  cout<<"The distance is ";
  cout<<dist << endl;
  return 0;
}
```

RESULTS
```
Enter the x coordinate for point 1: 5
Enter the y coordinate for point 1: 5
Enter the x coordinate for point 2: -5
Enter the y coordinate for point 2: -5
-10 vs -10
The distance is 12.34
```

Now, looking at the calculation for the distance, we can see that those intermediate values are in fact squared. Since we already know how to write a "square" function (from a previous chapter), let's do so. The following example shows the program with the "squaring" calculation performed.

```
#include <iostream>
#include <iomanip>
#include <string>
using namespace std;


int square(int what){
  int answer = what * what;
  return answer;
}

float distance(int x1, int y1, int x2, int y2) {
  int diffx, diffy, sqx, sqy;
  diffx = x2-x1;
  diffy = y2-y1;
  sqx = square(diffx);
  sqy = square(diffy);
  cout<<sqx << " vs ";
  cout<<sqy << endl;
  return 12.34;
}

int main() {
  int x1, y1, x2, y2;
  cout<<"Enter the x coordinate for point 1: ";
  cin>>x1;
  cout<<x1 << endl;
  cout<<"Enter the y coordinate for point 1: ";
  cin>>y1;
  cout<<y1 << endl;
  cout<<"Enter the x coordinate for point 2: ";
  cin>>x2;
  cout<<x2 << endl;
  cout<<"Enter the y coordinate for point 2: ";
  cin>>y2;
  cout<<y2 << endl;
  float dist = distance(x1, y1, x2, y2);
```

```
  cout<<"The distance is ";
  cout<<dist << endl;
  return 0;
}
```

RESULTS
```
Enter the x coordinate for point 1: 5
Enter the y coordinate for point 1: 5
Enter the x coordinate for point 2: -5
Enter the y coordinate for point 2: -5
100 vs 100
The distance is 12.34
```

Adding `sqx` and `sqy` together is easy; the following program shows this. For added variety, the distance function now returns the result of the addition. Note that everything is still an integer.

```
#include <iostream>
#include <iomanip>
#include <string>
using namespace std;

int square(int what){
  int answer = what * what;
  return answer;
}

float distance(int x1, int y1, int x2, int y2) {
  int diffx, diffy, sqx, sqy, total;
  diffx = x2-x1;
  diffy = y2-y1;
  sqx = square(diffx);
  sqy = square(diffy);
  total = sqx + sqy;
  return total;
}

int main() {
  int x1, y1, x2, y2;
  cout<<"Enter the x coordinate for point 1: ";
  cin>>x1;
  cout<<x1 << endl;
  cout<<"Enter the y coordinate for point 1: ";
  cin>>y1;
  cout<<y1 << endl;
  cout<<"Enter the x coordinate for point 2: ";
  cin>>x2;
  cout<<x2 << endl;
  cout<<"Enter the y coordinate for point 2: ";
  cin>>y2;
  cout<<y2 << endl;
  float dist = distance(x1, y1, x2, y2);
  cout<<"The distance is ";
  cout<<dist << endl;
  return 0;
}
```

RESULTS

```
Enter the x coordinate for point 1: 5
Enter the y coordinate for point 1: 5
Enter the x coordinate for point 2: -5
Enter the y coordinate for point 2: -5
The distance is 200
```

All that remains is to calculate the square root – but wait! We don't have anything with which to do that! It's true that in a fully functional professional environment we would have access to a square root function; however, since this book is meant to help you learn, let's develop our own. (It's not as hard as it might sound…)

First of all, we need to know how to calculate a square root. This turns out not to be too difficult if you have access to a computer programming language (which we do!). Doing a quick Internet search for "Babylonian square root method" you will likely come across something like the following:

$$x_{n+1} = \frac{1}{2}\left(x_n + \frac{S}{x_n}\right),$$

Source: http://en.wikipedia.org/wiki/Methods_of_computing_square_roots

Where x_n is your current "guess" and S is the number you're trying to take the square root of. Again, this might seem daunting, but it's easy if you take it in pieces. First, let's adjust the program to call a function called `squareRoot` and pass it a number. In this case, although our total is an integer, there is no reason to limit our `squareRoot` function to integers, so we will have the input parameter be a `float`. Let's set the "guess" to be half of S. The code so far is shown below:

```cpp
#include <iostream>
#include <iomanip>
#include <string>
using namespace std;


float squareRoot(float s) {
  float xn;
  xn = s / 2.0;
  return xn;
}

int square(int what){
  int answer = what * what;
  return answer;
}

float distance(int x1, int y1, int x2, int y2) {
  int diffx, diffy, sqx, sqy, total;
  diffx = x2-x1;
  diffy = y2-y1;
  sqx = square(diffx);
  sqy = square(diffy);
  total = sqx + sqy;
  float dist = squareRoot(total);
  return dist;
}
```

```
int main() {
  int x1, y1, x2, y2;
  cout<<"Enter the x coordinate for point 1: ";
  cin>>x1;
  cout<<x1 << endl;
  cout<<"Enter the y coordinate for point 1: ";
  cin>>y1;
  cout<<y1 << endl;
  cout<<"Enter the x coordinate for point 2: ";
  cin>>x2;
  cout<<x2 << endl;
  cout<<"Enter the y coordinate for point 2: ";
  cin>>y2;
  cout<<y2 << endl;
  float dist = distance(x1, y1, x2, y2);
  cout<<"The distance is ";
  cout<<dist << endl;
  return 0;
}
```

RESULTS
```
Enter the x coordinate for point 1: 5
Enter the y coordinate for point 1: 5
Enter the x coordinate for point 2: -5
Enter the y coordinate for point 2: -5
The distance is 100
```

Everything is working as planned, although dividing by 2 is a poor excuse for a square root function. The Babylonian method works by continuing to get closer and closer to the actual answer by successive approximation. Successive approximation just means trying over and over again, each time coming closer to the actual answer. Well, when you think of doing something over and over again in a program, of course the method will involve looping. For complex calculations with lots of significant digits, your program might have to loop quite a bit; however, for our purposes here it turns out that 10 loop iterations does a pretty good job. The following code shows the next stage in the development:

```
float squareRoot(float s) {
  float xn;
  xn = s / 2.0;
  int counter = 1;
  while (counter <= 10) {
    counter = counter + 1;
  }
  return xn;
}
```

Notice that nothing new actually happens here; all we've done is to add a loop that doesn't do anything; something is going to have to be inserted into the loop to make this work. Looking back at the calculation of the Babylonian square root approximation, we see that it's a simple calculation, involving only one addition and two divisions. The code below shows the entire algorithm implemented and running:

```
#include <iostream>
#include <iomanip>
#include <string>
```

```cpp
using namespace std;

float squareRoot(float s) {
    float xn;
    xn = s / 2.0;
    int counter = 1;
    while (counter <= 10) {
        xn = (xn + (s/xn))/2.0;
        cout<<"xn is now ";
        cout<<xn << endl;
        counter = counter + 1;
    }
    return xn;
}

int square(int what){
    int answer = what * what;
    return answer;
}

float distance(int x1, int y1, int x2, int y2) {
    int diffx, diffy, sqx, sqy, total;
    diffx = x2-x1;
    diffy = y2-y1;
    sqx = square(diffx);
    sqy = square(diffy);
    total = sqx + sqy;
    float dist = squareRoot(total);
    return dist;
}

int main() {
    int x1, y1, x2, y2;
    cout<<"Enter the x coordinate for point 1: ";
    cin>>x1;
    cout<<x1 << endl;
    cout<<"Enter the y coordinate for point 1: ";
    cin>>y1;
    cout<<y1 << endl;
    cout<<"Enter the x coordinate for point 2: ";
    cin>>x2;
    cout<<x2 << endl;
    cout<<"Enter the y coordinate for point 2: ";
    cin>>y2;
    cout<<y2 << endl;
    float dist = distance(x1, y1, x2, y2);
    cout<<"The distance is ";
    cout<<dist << endl;
    return 0;
}
```

RESULTS
```
Enter the x coordinate for point 1: 5
Enter the y coordinate for point 1: 5
Enter the x coordinate for point 2: -5
Enter the y coordinate for point 2: -5
xn is now 51
xn is now 27.4608
xn is now 17.3719
```

```
xn is now 14.4424
xn is now 14.1453
xn is now 14.1421
xn is now 14.1421
xn is now now 14.1421
xn is now 14.1421
xn is now 14.1421
The distance is 14.1421
```

The program above includes some trace statements to help you understand what is going on. Each time through the loop, the value of x_n gets closer and closer to the proper answer, which is approximately `14.1421356237309504880168887242097` – or 14.1421 as far as we are concerned, since this seems to be close enough! It is because of this rounding that we are able to run the algorithm only 10 times and get a "good enough" answer. If we were calculating a trajectory to Mars we would definitely want more than four decimal places of precision!

Test your program with other data

At this point you should verify that the program works with examples other than the one that was given. This is important because you may have inadvertently written something into the program that will only work for this example. Note also that it is always a good idea to test your program for the "zeroth" case – in this instance, that would be when both points were at the same coordinates, perhaps even both at the origin (0,0):

```
Enter the x coordinate for point 1: 0
Enter the y coordinate for point 1: 0
Enter the x coordinate for point 2: 0
Enter the y coordinate for point 2: 0
xn is now -nan
xn is now -nan
xn is now -nan
xn is now -nan
xn is now -nan
xn is now -nan
xn is now -nan
xn is now -nan
xn is now -nan
xn is now -nan
The distance is -nan
```

The key word `nan` stands for *not a number*. If you look carefully at the program you will be able to see the problem: `xn` is used as the denominator in the calculation of `squareRoot`, but if `s` is originally zero, this will cause `xn` to be zero and boom! we're dividing by zero again.

A fix is simple: if the number you are trying to get the square root of is zero, then the square root is just zero and there is no reason to calculate anything. The following code shows this simple fix, although students will sometimes make this harder than it really is. Remember: *In order to avoid having your program do something you do not want it to do, put a conditional statement in it to avoid that behavior.*

```
float squareRoot(float s) {
  float xn;
  if (s == 0.0) {
    return 0.0;
```

```
  }
  xn = s / 2.0;
  int counter = 1;
  while (counter <= 10) {
    xn = (xn + (s/xn))/2.0;
    counter = counter + 1;
  }
  return xn;
}
```

Once you have verified that the program seems to be operating correctly, it's a good idea to review it to see if there is something that you could do to make it better before sending it to your users (aka releasing it) – or, if you are a student, handing it in to your instructor.

Making your program better

We discussed earlier in the book that shorter programs are not always better programs; however, it is also true that we don't want programs that use unnecessary space or computational resources. In the case of the current extended example, we are using more memory than is needed because we have a few intermediate variables that really are not needed. The following code shows how you could reduce the number of intermediate variables:

Note that only a few computational cycles are saved because the calculations still need to be performed; however, the final version of the calculation is cleaner looking and somewhat more efficient. Remember, though, that sacrificing readability and maintainability for a few CPU cycles or a couple of bytes of RAM is typically not a good tradeoff. Also keep in mind that you need to re-test the program after making these types of changes in case you have inadvertently introduced an error into the code.

```
#include <iostream>
#include <iomanip>
#include <string>
using namespace std;

float squareRoot(float s) {
  float xn;
  if (s == 0.0) {
    return 0.0;
  }
  xn = s / 2.0;
  int counter = 1;
  while (counter <= 10) {
    xn = (xn + (s/xn))/2.0;
    counter = counter + 1;
  }
  return xn;
}

int square(int what){
  int answer = what * what;
  return answer;
}

float distance(int x1, int y1, int x2, int y2) {

  return (squareRoot(square(x2-x1) + square(y2-y1)));
```

```
}

int main() {
  int x1, y1, x2, y2;
  cout<<"Enter the x coordinate for point 1: ";
  cin>>x1;
  cout<<x1 << endl;
  cout<<"Enter the y coordinate for point 1: ";
  cin>>y1;
  cout<<y1 << endl;
  cout<<"Enter the x coordinate for point 2: ";
  cin>>x2;
  cout<<x2 << endl;
  cout<<"Enter the y coordinate for point 2: ";
  cin>>y2;
  cout<<y2 << endl;
  float dist = distance(x1, y1, x2, y2);
  cout<<"The distance is ";
  cout<<dist << endl;
  return 0;
}
```

RESULTS TEST 1
```
Enter the x coordinate for point 1: 0
Enter the y coordinate for point 1: 0
Enter the x coordinate for point 2: 0
Enter the y coordinate for point 2: 0
The distance is 0
```

RESULTS TEST 2
```
Enter the x coordinate for point 1: 5
Enter the y coordinate for point 1: 5
Enter the x coordinate for point 2: -5
Enter the y coordinate for point 2: -5
The distance is 14.1421
```

RESULTS TEST 3
```
Enter the x coordinate for point 1: 1
Enter the y coordinate for point 1: 2
Enter the x coordinate for point 2: 3
Enter the y coordinate for point 2: 4
The distance is 2.82843
```

Also, in the end, be sure to remove any remaining unnecessary trace statements from your code.

Summary

It is a truism in programming that all of the simple programs have already been written; thus it is important to realize that the examples in this book are simply scratching the surface of the complexity of generating professional programs. However, the basics that you are learning here are the basis for every program in existence. As the problems become more difficult, be sure to use the *spiral development* method – you will spend less time developing your programs and they will be better structured as well.

91

Exercises

Exercise 9.1. Using the Pythagorean Theorem, calculate the hypotenuse of a right triangle given the length of the two shorter sides. Be certain to use the square and squareRoot functions. Ask the user if s/he wants to keep entering data; if "Yes" then continue prompting and calculating. Assume no sides are negative. This might involve some research on your part! Use the following sample as a guide:

```
Enter side A: 3
Enter side B: 4
Side C is 5
Continue? Yes
Enter side A: 33
Enter side B: 44
Side C is 55
Continue? No
```

Exercise 9.2. The root mean square is a specific kind of average which is used for various purposes. It is given by the formula:

$$\sqrt{\frac{x_1^2 + x_2^2 + \ldots + x_n^2}{n}}$$

This means that a sequence of values is squared and summed, then divided by the count of the values; the entire calculation is then square-rooted. Ask the user for input; stop when the user enters -1. Use the following sample runs to design your program:

```
Enter a positive number: 1
Enter a positive number: 2
Enter a positive number: 3
Enter a positive number: 4
Enter a positive number: 5
Enter a positive number: -1
The root mean square is 3.32
```

The answer is calculated by calculating $(1^2 + 2^2 + 3^2 + 4^2 + 5^2)/5$ and then taking the square root of the result. Here is another example:

```
Enter a positive number: 88
Enter a positive number: 45
Enter a positive number: 37
Enter a positive number: 2
Enter a positive number: 55
Enter a positive number: 38
Enter a positive number: 96
Enter a positive number: 32
Enter a positive number: -1
The root mean square is 56.85
```

If there is no data available, you have to specify that:

```
Enter a positive number: -1
No data
```

Test your understanding

Be sure that you are able to explain the following concepts:

1. spiral development

2. Babylonian square root method

3. successive approxlmation

4. zeroth case

5. releasing

Chapter 10 – Using arrays

Although we have been able to produce some interesting applications using the material covered in this book, it may have occurred to you that the examples lacked a certain amount of power; they don't look like 21st century programming applications. One of the reasons for this is that most "real world" programming applications deal with lists of data, e.g. song playlists, addresses, things to do, calendar functions, etc. The most basic approach to storing data in a program is to use an *array*, which is an homogeneous, contiguous storage area in memory. *Homogeneous* here refers to the fact that all of the items in an array have to be the same type: `int`, `float`, or `string`. *Contiguous* means that the data are all lined up one next to the other; this is important because it allows us to process an array with a loop. The following program shows a simple application of an array:

```
#include <iostream>
#include <iomanip>
#include <string>
using namespace std;

int main() {
  int scores[4];
  scores[0] = 69;
  scores[1] = 79;
  scores[2] = 89;
  scores[3] = 99;
  cout<<"Your scores were: ";
  cout<<scores[0] << ", ";
  cout<<scores[1] << ", ";
  cout<<scores[2] << ", ";
  cout<<scores[3] << endl;
  return 0;
}
```

RESULTS
```
Your scores were: 69, 79, 89, 99
```

Note the following things about this program:

- At this point, there is not a great value in using an array for this application, so don't look too hard for one. It's just an example to get started. You could just as well have used four variables called score1 ... score4.

- You create an array with a similar approach to creating any other variable – it has to have a *type* and a *name*. The main difference is that you have to tell the compiler how many of these things (called *array elements*; in this case `scores`) you want.

- In this example, we simply assign values to the array and then display them one at a time. The true value of arrays is demonstrated when you combine them with loops, as is done in the next example.

Critically important!

Arrays start at zero, *not one* (called a *zero offset*). This is a constant source of confusion for introductory students. Just remember that an array of four elements goes from position 0 to position 3 (a total of four elements).

Looping the output

The following program demonstrates how to loop through the array to process the data. This is nice because no matter how many elements there are in the array, the number of lines needed to produce the output will be the same, even if there are 1000 elements in the array. Notice that we use the *loop control variable* to indicate what element of the array we wish to display. In this case we are using the loop counter as what is called the *array index*, which is always an integer.

```cpp
#include <iostream>
#include <iomanip>
#include <string>
using namespace std;

int main() {
  int scores[4];
  scores[0] = 69;
  scores[1] = 79;
  scores[2] = 89;
  scores[3] = 99;
  cout<<"Your scores were: ";
  int counter = 0;
  while (counter < 4) {
    cout<<scores[counter] << ", ";
    counter = counter + 1;
  }
  return 0;
}
```

RESULTS
```
Your scores were: 69, 79, 89, 99,
```

One small issue, though, is that the program displays an extra comma at the end of the output. This is easily fixed with an `if` statement, as shown below:

```cpp
#include <iostream>
#include <iomanip>
#include <string>
using namespace std;

int main() {
  int scores[4];
  scores[0] = 69;
  scores[1] = 79;
  scores[2] = 89;
  scores[3] = 99;
  cout<<"Your scores were: ";
  int counter = 0;
  while (counter < 4) {
```

```
    cout<<scores[counter];
    if (counter < 3) {
      cout  << ", ";
    }
    counter = counter + 1;
  }
  return 0;
}
```

RESULTS
```
Your scores were: 69, 79, 89, 99
```

With this example, though, we still use one line to fill each element of the array, which requires that we know the answers ahead of time. How about getting the data from the user instead? That is the purpose of the next example.

Getting array input from the user

The following program demonstrates how to get data from the user to *populate* (put data into) the array:

```
#include <iostream>
#include <iomanip>
#include <string>
using namespace std;

int main() {
  int scores[4];
  int counter = 0;
  while (counter < 4) {
    cout<<"Enter a score: ";
    cin>>scores[counter];
    cout<<scores[counter] << endl;
    counter = counter + 1;
  }
  cout<<"Your scores were: ";
  counter = 0;
  while (counter < 4) {
    cout<<scores[counter];
    if (counter < 3) {
      cout  << ", ";
    }
    counter = counter + 1;
  }
  return 0;
}
```

RESULTS
```
Enter a score: 69
Enter a score: 79
Enter a score: 89
Enter a score: 99
Your scores were: 69, 79, 89, 99
```

There are two loops: one for input and one for output; this isn't always necessary but it is quite common. Each of four times, the program will ask the user for a score and store it into the

97

next spot in the array. Using this approach, the program could easily be changed to handle, for example, ten scores by replacing all of the fours with tens in the program. But what if you don't know ahead of time how many scores there will be? This is the subject of the next example.

Processing an unknown number of inputs

It would be great to be able to just have the user keep adding elements to the array as long as there is data, and not have to know ahead of time exactly how many scores there were going to be. Unfortunately, it's a requirement that you pre-define the size of an array, and so you can't change the array if you've set the size to, say, ten, and the user wants to add fifteen. *(Actually, you can do this, but how is beyond the scope of this book.)* However, what you *can* do is to set the size of the array to be as large as you think the user will ever need, and just allow for the user to stop when s/he is out of data. The following program demonstrates how to do this:

```cpp
#include <iostream>
#include <iomanip>
#include <string>
using namespace std;

int main() {
   int scores[25];
   int counter = 0;
   string go_on = "yes";
   while (go_on == "yes") {
     cout<<"Enter a score (-1 to stop): ";
     cin>>scores[counter];
     cout<<scores[counter] << endl;
     if (scores[counter] == -1) {
       go_on = "no";
     }
     else {
       counter = counter + 1;
     }
   }
   cout<<"Your scores were: ";
   int counter2 = 0;
   while (counter2 < counter) {
     cout<<scores[counter2];
     if (counter2 < (counter-1)) {
       cout  << ", ";
     }
     counter2 = counter2 + 1;
   }
   return 0;
}
```

RESULTS
```
Enter a score (-1 to stop): 49
Enter a score (-1 to stop): 59
Enter a score (-1 to stop): 69
Enter a score (-1 to stop): 79
Enter a score (-1 to stop): 89
Enter a score (-1 to stop): 99
Enter a score (-1 to stop): -1
Your scores were: 49, 59, 69, 79, 89, 99
```

Note the following things about this program:

1. The array size is set to 25, which is a guess as to the maximum number of scores the user will want to add. More will be said about this later in the chapter.

2. We have to create our own loop control variable, called `go_on` here. This is initially set to `"yes"` and is changed to `"no"` when the user enters a `-1`.

3. We use `counter` to determine how many valid entries the user has entered. Note that if the user enters a `-1` then `counter` is not incremented. This means that the program will not display the `-1` to the screen when dumping the array contents.

Stopping the loop before too many items are entered

You may have noticed a design flaw in the above program. Even though we have created enough space for 25 elements, there is nothing stopping the user from continuing to enter scores past this number. If you run this program and enter 26 elements into the array, you are likely to see a run-time error; exactly how this will show up will vary based on what environment you're using.

Another possibility is that your program can fail but not tell you about it – this is called *failing silently*. This is a particularly insidious kind of error because it can go undetected all through development and testing and only show up after you have released the program to the public. When you hear in the news about some catastrophic software error bringing down a telephone network or something similar, it is often because of errors that lie dormant in software for a long time and then suddenly pop up under a specific set of circumstances. In our little example here, we need to add some protection (called an error trap) from this run-time error, as shown below.

```cpp
#include <iostream>
#include <iomanip>
#include <string>
using namespace std;

int main() {
  int scores[10];
  int counter = 0;
  string go_on = "yes";
  while (go_on == "yes") {
    if (counter >= 10) {
      cout<<"Out of array space!";
      cout<<endl;
      go_on = "no";
    }
    else {
      cout<<"Enter a score (-1 to stop): ";
      cin>>scores[counter];
      cout<<scores[counter] << endl;
      if (scores[counter] == -1) {
        go_on = "no";
      }
      else {
        counter = counter + 1;
      }
    }
  }
```

```
    }
    cout<<"Your scores were: ";
    int counter2 = 0;
    while (counter2 < counter) {
      cout<<scores[counter2];
      if (counter2 < (counter-1)) {
        cout  << ", ";
      }
      counter2 = counter2 + 1;
    }
    return 0;
}
```

RESULTS
```
Enter a score (-1 to stop): 1
Enter a score (-1 to stop): 2
Enter a score (-1 to stop): 3
Enter a score (-1 to stop): 4
Enter a score (-1 to stop): 5
Enter a score (-1 to stop): 6
Enter a score (-1 to stop): 7
Enter a score (-1 to stop): 8
Enter a score (-1 to stop): 9
Enter a score (-1 to stop): 10
Out of array space!
Your scores were: 1, 2, 3, 4, 5, 6, 7, 8, 9, 10
```

Note the following things about this program:

1. The array size has been changed to 10 to make the example fit on your screen.

2. When the loop is entered, `counter` is tested to make sure that it is in bounds. Checking afterwards does not make any sense (it would be too late!).

3. The loop stops if `counter` is greater than *or equal to* the array size. The reason for this is the zero offset – the array goes from position 0 to position 9 (10 elements total).

4. Note the following design pattern: If you want the program to do or not do something in a certain situation, just insert an `if` statement in the code. This is surprisingly hard for some students to incorporate into their toolbox of strategies, and yet it is fundamental to most programming problems.

Calculating statistics on the array

Finally, one of the major values of using an array is that you can fairly easily perform statistics on the data in the array. Note that if you can display the values of the array on the screen, you can also do math on them (if the values are numeric). For example, the program below shows the previous programs but with a total and average being calculated.

```
#include <iostream>
#include <iomanip>
#include <string>
using namespace std;
```

100

```
int main() {
  int scores[10];
  int counter = 0;
  int total = 0;
  string go_on = "yes";
  while (go_on == "yes") {
    if (counter >= 10) {
      cout<<"Out of array space!";
      cout<<endl;
      go_on = "no";
    }
    else {
      cout<<"Enter a score (-1 to stop): ";
      cin>>scores[counter];
      cout<<scores[counter] << endl;
      if (scores[counter] == -1) {
        go_on = "no";
      }
      else {
        total = total + scores[counter];
        counter = counter + 1;
      }
    }
  }
  cout<<"Your scores were: ";
  int counter2 = 0;
  while (counter2 < counter) {
    cout<<scores[counter2];
    if (counter2 < (counter-1)) {
      cout  << ", ";
    }
    counter2 = counter2 + 1;
  }
  cout<<endl;
  cout<<"There were " << counter;
  cout<<" data values." << endl;
  if (counter > 0){
    float average = total / counter;
    cout<<"The average was ";
    cout << average << endl;
  }
  return 0;
}
```

RESULTS
```
Enter a score (-1 to stop): 11
Enter a score (-1 to stop): 22
Enter a score (-1 to stop): 33
Enter a score (-1 to stop): 44
Enter a score (-1 to stop): 55
Enter a score (-1 to stop): -1
Your scores were: 11, 22, 33, 44, 55
There were 5 data values.
The average was 33
```

Note the following things:

1. We create a variable called `total` and initialize it to zero. Each time through the loop we add the next value from the array to total. In the end, this gives us the total of all of the values in the array. This is a standard approach to calculating anything you want on an array of numeric data values; you could use this same approach to calculate the standard deviation, the minimum and maximum values, etc.

2. Notice that the denominator of the average is just `counter` because we started at position zero. This helps to explain the answer to the oft-asked question: why do arrays start at position zero? The reason is that, once you get used to it, this approach makes a lot of other aspects of your programs more natural.

Summary

This chapter described how to define and use arrays, which are homogeneous, contiguous areas of memory used to store lists of related things. In addition, looping through the array for input, output and calculations was covered.

Exercises

Exercise 10.1. Write a program that asks the user for up to 10 integers (it could be fewer); stop prompting when the user enters zero. Then list the numbers in reverse order. Use the following example run as a guide.

```
Enter a number (0 to stop): 34
Enter a number (0 to stop): 87
Enter a number (0 to stop): 21
Enter a number (0 to stop): 98
Enter a number (0 to stop): 3
Enter a number (0 to stop): 0
Reverse order: 3, 98, 21, 87, 34
```

Exercise 10.2. Write a program that collects weights and stores them in an array of floats. Assume that there will not be more than 20. Keep track of the highest weight entered. When the user enters a weight of 0 (zero) stop asking. Use the following run as a guide.

```
Enter a weight (zero to stop): 33.3
Enter a weight (zero to stop): 66.6
Enter a weight (zero to stop): 22.2
Enter a weight (zero to stop): 77.7
Enter a weight (zero to stop): 11.1
Enter a weight (zero to stop): 0
The maximum was 77.7
```

Test your understanding

Be sure that you are able to explain the following concepts:

1. array

2. homogeneous

3. contiguous

4. array elements

5. zero offset

6. array index

7. populate

8. failing silently

9. error trap

Chapter 11 – Some other useful features of C++

Everything you've learned until now is standard C++, although a stripped down version. Remember that there are five points that introductory students get stuck on: variables, conditionals, loops, functions, and arrays. Focusing just on these aspects of C++ up until now, without a lot of excess baggage, allows you, the new programmer , to focus on these concepts before getting involved in all the trappings of full-bore C++. Eventually, though, everyone will need to use the rest of the language, and that is the subject of this chapter.

Some details about strings

We've used strings in the previous examples, but not very much. The reason is that they can be a little bit confusing, and the idea behind this gentle introduction was to keep the amount of confusion to a minimum. Following is a simple program using strings:

```
#include <iostream>
#include <string>
using namespace std;

int main() {
  string message;
  message = "Hi there from the author!";
  cout<<"The message is: ";
  cout<<message << endl;
  return 0;
}
```

RESULTS
```
The message is: Hi there from the author!
```

Recall that to use strings in a program, you have have the `#include<string>` command near the top of the program. Note that the quotation marks do not show up in the program output; they are there to delimit where the text begins and ends. One question we did not deal with previously is: *how do I get the quotes to appear in the text?* One does this by inserting slashes in front of an extra pair of quotation marks in the program, as shown below:

```
#include <iostream>
#include <string>
using namespace std;

int main() {
  string message;
  message = "\"Hi there from the author!\"";
  cout<<"The message is: ";
  cout<<message << endl;
  return 0;
}
```

RESULTS
```
The message is: "Hi there from the author!"
```

String input in C++ has one nuance from which you were shielded in the previous examples. When using string values, you have to do something a little different; the following program shows how to handle this.

```cpp
#include <iostream>
#include <string>
using namespace std;

int main() {
  string message;
  cout<<"What is the message? ";
  getline(cin, message);
  cout<<"The message is: ";
  cout<<message << endl;
  return 0;
}
```

RESULTS
```
What is the message?
The message is: Hello there from user input!
```

Note that instead of using `cin << message;`, you use a new program structure – a function call – which looks like this: `getline(cin, fullName)`.

Unfortunately, this is not all there is to it. When programming in C++, if you read in a number (finishing by pressing the **enter** key), then C++ will leave the equivalent of the **enter** key (called a *control character*) in the input list to be processed later. (The input list is more formally called the *input buffer*.) Here is the problem: when you want to read a string, it is terminated (ended) with the **enter** key, so C++ reads the left over control character from the previous input as the end of the string you are trying to read and essentially skips your input. To see this problem in action, compile and run the following program using the input values `21` for `age` and `Bob Johnson` for `name`:

```cpp
#include <iostream>
#include <string>
using namespace std;

int main() {
  int age;
  string name;
  cout<<"What is your age? ";
  cin>>age;
  cout<<"What is your name? ";
  getline(cin, name);
  cout<<"Your age is: ";
  cout<<age << endl;
  cout<<"Your name is: ";
  cout<<name << endl;
  return 0;
}
```

RESULTS
```
What is your age? What is your name? Your age is: 21
Your name is:
```

It's hard to demonstrate this in a book, but if you run it you will see that the program skips over waiting for the user to enter the name! In order to fix this, you have to remove the control character from the input buffer, as shown below:

```cpp
#include <iostream>
#include <string>
using namespace std;

int main() {
  int age;
  string name;
  cout<<"What is your age? ";
  cin>>age;
  cin.ignore(); // <-- removes the control character!
  cout<<"What is your name? ";
  getline(cin, name);
  cout<<"Your age is: ";
  cout<<age << endl;
  cout<<"Your name is: ";
  cout<<name << endl;
  return 0;
}
```

RESULTS
```
What is your age? What is your name? Your age is: 21
Your name is: Bob Johnson
```

Note the line in the program that says `cin.ignore();`. This line calls a function that removes the extra control character from the input buffer. Note that if you are writing programs in C++ that you will have to keep the extra control character issue in mind, otherwise your program might not operate correctly (i.e., cause a run-time error or "bug").

Comments

We briefly touched on comments earlier in the text, but note the commment on the same line as the `cin.ignore();` in the previous program. Recall that a comment is a message left by a programmer, for a programmer – either the original author or programmers yet to come. Comments have several uses; in this case, a comment is used to explain what this line does in the program. This way, if you come back to the program months later the comment will remind you what you were doing. If, on the other hand, someone else was maintaining your program and was not familiar with cin.ignore(), then the comment would explain what it was doing there. A comment is started with two slash characters in a row (//) and ends at the end of the line they are on.

Remember that *comments don't execute!* Anything that is within a comment marker will not be read by the compiler and will not execute. This makes comments useful for making blocks of code inoperable when testing or fixing (aka debugging) a program.

else if statements

C++ allows a modification of the standard `if..else` statement called the `else if` statement. Theoretically this does the same thing as an `else` followed by an `if`; however, it makes certain kinds of programs easier to write and understand. Consider the program which calculates a person's BMI, as was done in an exercise earlier in the book:

```cpp
#include <iostream>
#include <string>
using namespace std;

int main() {
  float bmi;
  cout<<"What is the BMI? ";
  cin>>bmi;
  cout<<bmi << endl;
  if (bmi >= 30) {
    cout<<"Obsese" << endl;
  }
  else if ((bmi >= 25) && (bmi < 30)) {
    cout<<"Overweight" << endl;
  }
  else if ((bmi >= 18.5) && (bmi < 25)) {
    cout<<"Normal" << endl;
  }
  else {
    cout<<"Underweight" << endl;
  }
  return 0;
}
```

RESULTS
```
What is the BMI? 21
Normal
```

Note that the `else if` construct allows you to keep all of the conditions on the same indentation level, which makes them more obviously related to one another. The use of `else if` in the program ensures that if, for example, a person's BMI is over 30, then none of the other tests (i.e., for overweight, normal, or underweight) will be executed. Here is an example of where knowing something about who will be using the program is a good thing. For example, if this program will be used on a weight reduction web site, probably more people who use it will be overweight than underweight; so it's a good idea to test for the higher numbers first to speed up the execution of the program.

This program could also be done with `else` statements with nested `if` statements. The following program shows how this would look. Note that it's harder to read this program because of all the indentations. Heavily nested statements are hard to read and should be avoided – using `else if` statements can help.

```cpp
#include <iostream>
#include <string>
using namespace std;

int main() {
  float bmi;
  cout<<"What is the BMI? ";
  cin>>bmi;
  cout<<bmi << endl;
  if (bmi >= 30) {
```

```
      cout<<"Obsese" << endl;
    }
  else {
    if ((bmi >= 25) && (bmi < 30)) {
      cout<<"Overweight" << endl;
    }
    else {
      if ((bmi >= 18.5) && (bmi < 25)) {
        cout<<"Normal" << endl;
      }
      else {
        cout<<"Underweight" << endl;
      }
    }
  }
  return 0;
}
```

RESULTS
```
What is the BMI? 11
Underweight
```

Other kinds of loops

C++ allows you to use two other kinds of loops, called `for` loops and `do..while` loops. Although these constructs are useful in professional programming, they are not strictly necessary and experience shows that students often become confused when using them. Thus they are not covered in this textbook, under the theory that it's better to know one looping method really well rather than know three somewhat and be confused. Again, it's important to understand that there isn't anything the other looping constructs can do that you can't do with a `while` loop.

Built-in functions

C++ contains hundreds of built-in functions for doing various things, especially math. The following table shows some of the more common ones. In order to use these functions, you will usually need to include a *header file* at the top; the functions shown below need the line `#include <cmath>` near the top of the program.

Function name	Description	Parameters	Return type
pow	**Raise** base to the power of exp	base: double exp:double	double
sqrt	Returns the square root of p1	p1: double	double
ceil	Round up p1	p1: double	int
floor	Round down p1	p1: double	int
fabs	Absolute value of p1	p1: double	double

Note that a `double` is a *double precision* `float`, which means that it can store approximately twice as many significant digits as a `float`. In practice, it's often best to simply use `double` for all of your floating point variables.

Here is an example program using a built-in mathematical function:

```
#include <iostream>
#include <cmath>
using namespace std;

int main() {
  double answer;
  answer = sqrt(82.3);
  cout<<"The square root of 82.3 is ";
  cout<<answer << endl;
  return 0;
}
```

RESULTS
```
The square root of 82.3 is 9.07193
```

Conclusion

This chapter gave you a glimpse of the "further reaches of C++" so to speak. If you are interested to pursue your education further, there are a number of books on C++ available on Amazon. As stated at the outset, experience shows that those books quickly get mired in details and are confusing to novices; however, with your experience using this text, you should be ready to tackle those larger tomes! Good luck, and good programming!

Solutions to exercises

Exercise 1.1

```cpp
#include <iostream>
#include <string>
using namespace std;

int main() {
  cout<<"Hello Universe! ";
  return 0;
}
```

RESULTS
```
Hello Universe!
```

Exercise 1.2

```cpp
#include <iostream>
#include <string>
using namespace std;

int main() {
  cout<<"Hello, there World! ";
  return 0;
}
```

RESULTS
```
Hello, there World!
```

Exercise 1.3

```cpp
#include <iostream>
#include <string>
using namespace std;

int main() {
  cout<<"Hello, there! ";
  cout<<endl;
  cout<<"How are you? ";
  cout<<endl;
  return 0;
}
```

RESULTS
```
Hello, there!
How are you?
```

Exercise 1.4

```
#include <iostream>
#include <string>
using namespace std;

int main() {
  cout<<"abcdefghijklm";
  cout<<endl;
  cout<<"nopqrstuvwxyz";
  cout<<endl;
  return 0;
}
```

RESULTS
```
abcdefghijklm
nopqrstuvwxyz
```

Exercise 1.5

```
#include <iostream>
#include <string>
using namespace std;

int main() {
  cout<<"abcdefghijklm";
  cout<<"nopqrstuvwxyz";
  cout<<endl;
  return 0;
}
```

RESULTS
```
abcdefghijklmnopqrstuvwxyz
```

Exercise 2.1

```
#include <iostream>
#include <string>
using namespace std;

int main() {
  int length;
  int width;
  int height;
  cout<<"Enter length: ";
  cin>>length;
  cout<<length;
  cout<<endl;
  cout<<"Enter width: ";
  cin>>width;
  cout<<width;
  cout<<endl;
```

```
  cout<<"Enter height: ";
  cin>>height;
  cout<<height;
  cout<<endl;
  int volume = length * (width * height);
  cout<<"The volume is ";
  cout<<volume;
  cout<<endl;
  return 0;
}
```

RESULTS
```
Enter length: 1
Enter width: 2
Enter height: 3
The volume is 6
```

Exercise 2.2

```
#include <iostream>
#include <string>
using namespace std;

int main() {
  int r;
  cout<<"Enter radius: ";
  cin>>r;
  cout<<r;
  cout<<endl;
  int answer = (((r * (r * r)) * 4) * 3.1415)/3;
  cout<<"The volume is ";
  cout<<answer;
  cout<<endl;
  return 0;
}
```

RESULTS
```
Enter radius: 21
The volume is 38791
```

Exercise 2.3

```
#include <iostream>
#include <string>
using namespace std;

int main() {
  int f;
  cout<<"Temp in Fahrenheit: ";
  cin>>f;
  cout<<f;
  cout<<endl;
```

113

```
  int answer = ((f-32)*5)/9;
  cout<<"The temp in Celcius is ";
  cout<<answer;
  cout<<endl;
  return 0;
}
```

RESULTS

```
Temp in Fahrenheit: 82
The temp in Celcius is 27
```

Exercise 2.4

```
#include <iostream>
#include <string>
using namespace std;

int main() {
  int c;
  cout<<"Temp in Celcius ";
  cin>>c;
  cout<<c;
  cout<<endl;
  int answer = ((9*c)/5)+32;
  cout<<"The temp in Fahrenheit is ";
  cout<<answer;
  cout<<endl;
  return 0;
}
```

RESULTS

```
Temp in Celcius 27
The temp in Fahrenheit is 80
```

Exercise 3.1

```
#include <iostream>
#include <string>
using namespace std;

int main() {
  string name;
  cout<<"What is your name? ";
  cin>>name;
  cout<<"Hello, ";
  cout<<name;
  cout<<"!";
  cout<<endl;
  return 0;
}
```

What is your name? Hello, Adam!

Exercise 3.2

```cpp
#include <iostream>
#include <string>
using namespace std;

int main() {
  string lname;
  cout<<"What is your last name? ";
  cin>>lname;
  cout<<lname;
  cout<<endl;

  int age;
  cout<<"What is your age? ";
  cin>>age;
  cout<<age;
  cout<<endl;

  cout<<"Your userid is ";
  cout<<lname;
  cout<<age;
  cout<<endl;

  return 0;
}
```

RESULTS
What is your last name? Jones
What is your age? 20
Your userid is Jones20

Exercise 3.3

```cpp
#include <iostream>
#include <string>
using namespace std;

int main() {
  string major;
  cout<<"What is your major? ";
  cin>>major;
  cout<<major;
  cout<<endl;

  float gpa;
  cout<<"What is your gpa ";
  cin>>gpa;
  cout<<gpa;
  cout<<endl;
```

```
  cout<<major;
  cout<<" is very hard. Why do you ";
  cout<<" think you have a GPA of  ";
  cout<<gpa;
  cout<<"?";
  cout<<endl;

  return 0;
}
```

RESULTS
```
What is your major? Biology
What is your gpa 3.56
Biology is very hard. Why do you  think you have a GPA of  3.56?
```

Exercise 4.1

```
#include <iostream>
#include <string>
using namespace std;

int main() {
  int grade;
  cout<<"Enter a grade: ";
  cin>>grade;
  cout<<grade;
  cout<<endl;

  if (grade >= 90) {
    cout<<"A";
  }
  if (grade < 90) {
    if (grade >= 80) {
      cout<<"B";
    }
  }
  if (grade < 80) {
    if (grade >= 70) {
      cout<<"C";
    }
  }
  if (grade < 70) {
    if (grade >= 60) {
      cout<<"D";
    }
  }
  if (grade < 60) {
    cout<<"F";
  }
  return 0;
}
```

RESULTS (run #1)
```
Enter a grade: 90
```

A

RESULTS (run #2)
Enter a grade: 80
B

RESULTS (run #3)
Enter a grade: 70
C

RESULTS (run #4)
Enter a grade: 60
D

RESULTS (run #5)
Enter a grade: 59
F

Exercise 4.2

```cpp
#include <iostream>
#include <string>
using namespace std;

int main() {
  int bmi;
  cout<<"Enter BMI: ";
  cin>>bmi;
  cout<<bmi;
  cout<<endl;

  if (bmi < 18) {
    cout<<"Underweight";
  }
  if (bmi >= 18) {
    if (bmi <= 24) {
      cout<<"Normal";
    }
  }
  if (bmi >= 25) {
    if (bmi <= 30) {
      cout<<"Overweight";
    }
  }
  if (bmi >= 31) {
    cout<<"Obese";
  }

  return 0;
}
```

RESULTS (run #1)
Enter BMI: 17
Underweight

RESULTS (run #2)
Enter BMI: 18

117

Normal

RESULTS (run #3)
Enter BMI: 24
Normal

RESULTS (run #4)
Enter BMI: 25
Overweight

RESULTS (run #5)
Enter BMI: 30
Overweight

RESULTS (run #6)
Enter BMI: 31
Obese

Exercise 5.1

```cpp
#include <iostream>
#include <string>
using namespace std;

int main() {
  int grade;
  cout<<"Enter a grade: ";
  cin>>grade;
  cout<<grade;
  cout<<endl;

  if (grade >= 90) {
    cout<<"A";
  }
  else {
    if (grade >= 80) {
      cout<<"B";
    }
    else {
      if (grade >= 70) {
        cout<<"C";
      }
      else {
        if (grade >= 60) {
          cout<<"D";
        }
        else{
          cout<<"F";
        }
      }
    }
  }
  return 0;
}
```

RESULTS (run #1)
Enter a grade: 90
A

Exercise 5.2

```
#include <iostream>
#include <string>
using namespace std;

int main() {
  int bmi;
  cout<<"Enter BMI: ";
  cin>>bmi;
  cout<<bmi;
  cout<<endl;

  if (bmi < 18) {
    cout<<"Underweight";
  }
  else {
    if (bmi <= 24) {
      cout<<"Normal";
    }
    else{
      if (bmi <= 30) {
        cout<<"Overweight";
      }
      else {
        cout<<"Obese";
      }
    }
  }
  return 0;
}
```

RESULTS (run #1)
Enter BMI: 17
Underweight

RESULTS (run #2)
Enter BMI: 18
Normal

RESULTS (run #3)

119

Enter BMI: 24
Normal

RESULTS (run #4)
Enter BMI: 25
Overweight

RESULTS (run #5)
Enter BMI: 30
Overweight

RESULTS (run #6)
Enter BMI: 31
Obese

Exercise 6.1

```
#include <iostream>
#include <string>
using namespace std;

int main() {
  int num;
  int total = 0;
  while (total < 22) {
    cout<<"Please enter a number between 1 and 11: ";
    cin>>num;
    cout<<num;
    cout<<endl;
    if ((num < 1) || (num > 11)) {
      cout<<"Out of range; rejected.";
      cout<<endl;
    }
    else {
      total = total + num;
    }
  }
  cout<<"The total is ";
  cout<<total << endl;;
  return 0;
}
```

RESULTS
Please enter a number between 1 and 11: 4
Please enter a number between 1 and 11: 12
Out of range; rejected.
Please enter a number between 1 and 11: -1
Out of range; rejected.
Please enter a number between 1 and 11: 9
Please enter a number between 1 and 11: 8
Please enter a number between 1 and 11: 7
The total is 28

Exercise 6.2

```cpp
#include <iostream>
#include <string>
using namespace std;

int main() {
  int rows, cols, size;
  cout<<"Enter size: ";
  cin>>size;
  cout<<size;
  cout<<endl;
  rows = 0;
  while (rows < size) {
    cols = 0;
    while (cols <= rows) {
      cout<<"*";
      cols = cols + 1;
    }
    rows = rows + 1;
    cout<<endl;;
  }
  return 0;
}
```

RESULTS
```
Enter size: 5
*
**
***
****
*****
```

Exercise 7.1

```cpp
#include <iostream>
#include <string>
using namespace std;

int main() {
  int answer = 9999;
  int numEven = 0, numOdd = 0;
  int numPos =0, numNeg = 0;
  while (answer != 0) {
    cin>>answer;
    cout<<answer << endl;
    if (answer != 0) {
      if ((answer % 2) == 0) {
        numEven = numEven + 1;
      }
      if ((answer % 2) != 0) {
        numOdd = numOdd + 1;
      }
      if (answer < 0) {
        numNeg = numNeg + 1;
```

```
    }
    if (answer > 0) {
      numPos = numPos + 1;
    }
  }
}
cout<<"You entered: " << endl;
cout<<numEven << " even numbers" << endl;
cout<<numOdd << " odd numbers" << endl;
cout<<numPos << " positive numbers" << endl;
cout<<numNeg << " negative numbers" << endl;
return 0;
}
```

RESULTS

```
-1
1
-2
2
-3
3
0
You entered:
2 even numbers
4 odd numbers
3 positive numbers
3 negative numbers
```

Exercise 7.2

```
#include <iostream>
#include <string>
using namespace std;

int main() {
  int x, y;
  cout<<"Enter x: ";
  cin>>x;
  cout<<x << endl;
  cout<<"Enter y: ";
  cin>>y;
  cout<<y << endl;
  if ((x == 0) || (y == 0)) {
    cout<<"Axis points are skipped." << endl;
  }
  else {
    if ((x > 0) && (y > 0)) {
      cout<<"Quadrant I" << endl;
    }
    if ((x < 0) && (y > 0)) {
      cout<<"Quadrant II" << endl;
    }
    if ((x < 0) && (y < 0)) {
      cout<<"Quadrant III" << endl;
    }
    if ((x > 0) && (y < 0)) {
      cout<<"Quadrant IV" << endl;
```

```
      }
    }
    return 0;
}
```

RESULTS (run #1)
```
Enter x: 1
Enter y: 1
Quadrant I
```

RESULTS (run #2)
```
Enter x: -1
Enter y: 1
Quadrant II
```

RESULTS (run #3)
```
Enter x: -1
Enter y: -1
Quadrant III
```

RESULTS (run #4)
```
Enter x: 1
Enter y: -1
Quadrant IV
```

Exercise 8.1

```cpp
#include <iostream>
#include <string>
using namespace std;

string evenOrOdd(int number) {
  string answer;
  if ((number % 2) == 0) {
    answer = "Even";
  }
  else {
    answer = "Odd";
  }
  return answer;
}

int main() {
  string answer;
  int number = 1;
  while (number != 0) {
    cout<<"Enter a number: ";
    cin>>number;
    cout<<number;
    if (number != 0) {
      answer = evenOrOdd(number);
      cout<<" is " << answer << endl;
```

```
    }
  }
  return 0;
}
```

```
Enter a number: 1 is Odd
Enter a number: 2 is Even
Enter a number: 3 is Odd
Enter a number: 4 is Even
Enter a number: 5 is Odd
Enter a number: 0
```

Exercise 8.2

```
#include <iostream>
#include <string>
using namespace std;

int sumTo(int number) {
  int counter = 1;
  int total = 0;
  while (counter <= number) {
    total = total + counter;
    counter = counter + 1;
  }
  return total;
}

int main() {
  int answer;
  int number = 1;
  while (number != 0) {
    cout<<"Enter a number: ";
    cin>>number;
    cout<<number;
    if (number != 0) {
      answer = sumTo(number);
      cout<<" sums to " << answer << endl;
    }
  }
  return 0;
}
```

RESULTS
```
Enter a number: 5 sums to 15
Enter a number: 25 sums to 325
Enter a number: 100 sums to 5050
Enter a number: 0
```

124

Exercise 9.1

```cpp
#include <iostream>
#include <string>
using namespace std;

float squareRoot(float s) {
  float xn;
  if (s == 0) {
    xn = 0;
  }
  else {
    xn = s / 2.0;
    int counter = 1;
    while (counter <= 10) {
      xn = (xn + (s/xn)) / 2.0;
      counter = counter + 1;
    }
  }
  return xn;
}

int square(int what) {
  return what*what;
}

int main() {
  float sideA, sideB, sideC;
  string answer = "yes";
  while (answer == "yes") {
    cout<<"Enter side A: ";
    cin>>sideA;
    cout<<sideA << endl;
    cout<<"Enter side B: ";
    cin>>sideB;
    cout<<sideB << endl;
    sideC = squareRoot(square(sideA)+square(sideB));
    cout<<"Side C is " << sideC << endl;
    cout<<"Continue? ";
    cin>>answer;
    cout<<answer << endl;
  }
  return 0;
}
```

RESULTS
```
Enter side A: 3
Enter side B: 4
Side C is 5
Continue? yes
Enter side A: 33
Enter side B: 44
Side C is 55
Continue? no
```

Exercise 9.2

```cpp
#include <iostream>
#include <string>
using namespace std;

float squareRoot(float s) {
  float xn;
  if (s == 0) {
    xn = 0;
  }
  else {
    xn = s / 2.0;
    int counter = 1;
    while (counter <= 10) {
      xn = (xn + (s/xn)) / 2.0;
      counter = counter + 1;
    }
  }
  return xn;
}

int square(int what) {
  return what*what;
}

int main() {
  int num = 1, count = 0;
  float total = 0;
  while (num > 0) {
    cout<<"Enter a positive number: ";
    cin>>num;
    cout<<num << endl;
    if (num > 0) {
      int squared = square(num);
      total = total + squared;
      count = count + 1;
    }
  }
  if (count == 0) {
    cout<<"No data" << endl;
  }
  else {
    float rms, div;
    div = total / count;
    rms = squareRoot(div);
    cout<<"The root mean square is ";
    cout<<rms << endl;
  }
  return 0;
}
```

RESULTS (run #1)
```
Enter a positive number: 1
Enter a positive number: 2
Enter a positive number: 3
Enter a positive number: 4
Enter a positive number: 5
```

126

```
Enter a positive number: -1
The root mean square is 3.31662
```

RESULTS (run #2)
```
Enter a positive number: 88
Enter a positive number: 45
Enter a positive number: 37
Enter a positive number: 2
Enter a positive number: 55
Enter a positive number: 38
Enter a positive number: 96
Enter a positive number: 32
Enter a positive number: -1
The root mean square is 56.8452
```

RESULTS (run #3)
```
Enter a positive number: -1
No data
```

Exercise 10.1

```cpp
#include <iostream>
#include <string>
using namespace std;

int main() {
  int numbers[10];
  int counter = 0;
  string go_on = "yes";
  while (go_on == "yes") {
    cout<<"Enter a number (0 to stop): ";
    if (counter >= 10) {
      cout<<"Out of array spaces!" << endl;
      go_on = "no";
    }
    else {
      cin>>numbers[counter];
      cout<<numbers[counter] << endl;
      if (numbers[counter] != 0) {
        counter = counter + 1;
      }
      else {
        go_on = "no";
      }
    }
  }
  int counter2 = counter-1;
  int total = 0;
  cout<<"Your numbers in reverse order are: ";
  cout<<endl;
  while (counter2 >= 0) {
    cout<<numbers[counter2];
    if (counter2 > 0) {
      cout<<", ";
```

127

```
    }
    counter2 = counter2 - 1;
  }
  cout<<endl;
  return 0;
}
```

RESULTS
```
Enter a number (0 to stop): 11
Enter a number (0 to stop): 33
Enter a number (0 to stop): 55
Enter a number (0 to stop): 77
Enter a number (0 to stop): 99
Enter a number (0 to stop): 0
Your numbers in reverse order are:
99, 77, 55, 33, 11
```

Exercise 10.2

```
#include <iostream>
#include <string>
using namespace std;

int main() {
  float weights[20];
  float maximum;
  int counter = 0;
  string go_on = "yes";
  while (go_on == "yes") {
    cout<<"Enter a weight (0 to stop): ";
    if (counter >= 20) {
      cout<<"Out of array spaces!" << endl;
      go_on = "no";
    }
    else {
      cin>>weights[counter];
      cout<<weights[counter] << endl;
      if (counter == 0) {
        maximum = weights[counter];
      }
      if (weights[counter] != 0) {
        if (weights[counter] > maximum){
          maximum = weights[counter];
        }
        counter = counter + 1;
      }
      else {
        go_on = "no";
      }
    }
  }
  cout<<"The maximum was ";
  cout<<maximum << endl;
  return 0;
}
```

128

RESULTS
```
Enter a weight (0 to stop): 33.3
Enter a weight (0 to stop): 66.6
Enter a weight (0 to stop): 22.2
Enter a weight (0 to stop): 77.7
Enter a weight (0 to stop): 11.1
Enter a weight (0 to stop): 0
The maximum was 77.7
```

Appendix A - Choosing and using an IDE

A C++ program takes commands that you enter in text and allows you to execute those commands on your computer. There are several steps involved in this process:

1. Create a text file that contains a valid C++ program.

2. Use a software program called a compiler; a compiler is a program used to translate the text program into a format that your computer can understand (called machine code).

3. Run the program.

Many programmers use a software package called an *interactive development environment (IDE)*, which makes the above steps easier. An *IDE* is a program which allows you to write, run and debug your programs all from a consistent interface. The word *interface* means the way the program is displayed and how the user interacts with it.

After using a web-based compiler such as Ideone for awhile, you will probably want to install and use a client-based IDE. Some free possibilities (as of this writing) include the following; use your favorite search engine to find them:

- Microsoft Visual Studio Express

- Eclipse IDE for C++

- GCC (also known as g++)

Some of these are easier to install than others, and some are limited to one operating system or another (e.g., Windows or OSX). Also try searching Youtube for videos on how to install and use the compiler.

24996569R00078

Made in the USA
San Bernardino, CA
08 February 2019